laughing

at my

nightmare

laughing

at my

nightmare

shane
burcaw

roaring brook press

new york

Library of Congress Cataloging-in-Publication Data

Burcaw, Shane.
    Laughing at my nightmare / Shane Burcaw. — First edition.
        pages cm
    Audience: 12+
    Summary: "With acerbic wit and a hilarious voice, Shane Burcaw's YA
memoir describes the challenges he faces as a 20-year-old with spinal
muscular atrophy. From awkward handshakes to trying to finding a girlfriend
and everything in between"—Provided by publisher.
    ISBN 978-1-62672-007-7 (hardback) — ISBN 978-1-62672-008-4 (ebook)
1. Burcaw, Shane,—Health. 2. Spinal muscular atrophy—Patients—United
States—Biography. 3. People with disabilities—United States—Juvenile
literature. I. Title.
    RC935.A8B87 2014
    617.4'82044092—dc23
    [B]
                                                         2014010634

Roaring Brook Press books may be purchased for business or promotional use.
For information on bulk purchases please contact Macmillan Corporate and
Premium Sales Department at (800) 221-7945 x5442 or by email at
specialmarkets@macmillan.com.

First edition 2014
Book design by Andrew Arnold
Printed in the United States of America

5 7 9 10 8 6 4

To my mom, Sue;
my dad, Jon;
and my brother, Andrew.

I fucking love you guys.

introduction

The forest of pube-y leg hair sprouting from my brother's calf bristles the tip of my nose as he stands over me on the floor of our rented minibus, yanking my shorts off. I try not to laugh, since my bladder is on the verge of exploding after seventeen hours of driving down the East Coast of the United States. Until now, I have chosen to hold my pee despite stopping at multiple rest areas along the way. Highway bathrooms tend to be pretty shitty for people in wheelchairs and I can't sit on a normal toilet, so when I have to pee, I use a travel urinal that someone holds under my penis. I have to be lying down to do this, and the floor of a highway restroom is by far the least desirable place to lie in the entire world. So there I lie, in the tightly cramped quarters of our tour bus in the parking lot of a Wendy's in Daytona Beach at two in the morning while Andrew maneuvers my penis into the little red travel urinal that I carry everywhere I go. We would have a lot more room if it weren't for the three cameramen surrounding us, capturing every angle of this intimate moment. I close my eyes, attempting not to accidentally make eye contact with a member of the film crew. Making eye contact will disrupt my stream.

It probably looks like we are filming a multi-fetish porno involving severely disabled people and urination. The back of the van is wide open, and I worry that a stranger might walk by. Although I guess it wouldn't be the worst thing that could happen. Besides, I'm used to people staring really hard at me. Whenever I'm out in public, it is pretty much a guarantee that several people will make it completely obvious that they have never seen someone like me before. By "someone like me" I mean an alien-like pterodactyl creature with a human head that uses a wheelchair. Okay, that's a slight exaggeration, but I must look awfully messed up if the looks I receive are any indication.

Because of a neuromuscular disease I've had since birth, my arms and legs are slightly fatter than a hot dog. My elbows and wrists are extremely atrophied; they look exactly like Tyrannosaurus Rex arms when I hold them against my chest. I am a few inches shy of five feet, and when I sit in my chair, it seems like I'm even shorter. My head is normal human size, which looks ridiculously funny/creepy sitting on top of my tiny body. Imagine a bobblehead doll in a wheelchair. I don't even blame people for staring. If I were a stranger, I would probably stare at me, too.

Over the years, I have gone through many methods for dealing with people who stare at me. When I was younger, I used to make scary faces at other little kids who were mesmerized by my chair because I got a kick out of their reactions. During middle school, I went through a stage where the constant stares really got under my skin. I remember doing things like approaching people who stared to ask them what they were looking at, pretending to cry to make an onlooker feel like a terrible person, and outright lying to people who had the balls to ask me questions about my disability. I would tell people that I was in a car accident that killed my whole family. I was young and stupid then and didn't know how to handle my situation.

I eventually got over my aversion of being stared at, which is why I am now okay with being filmed as a part of a documentary about the inaugural speaking tour of my nonprofit organization, Laughing At My Nightmare, Inc. It is only our first day on the road, and I am already discovering how ridiculous the upcoming week is going to be. When the pee jar is full, my brother hops out and rinses it out in the parking lot with half a bottle of Gatorade. Wendy's is closed at 2 a.m., and none of us wants to be in a van with a jarful of stench.

My mom would have a heart attack watching us improvise ways to take care of me on the road. But she is a thousand miles away at our home in Bethlehem, Pennsylvania, along with my dad. For the first time in my life, I am free.

This has not been the case for most of my life. I was born with spinal muscular atrophy, a disease that basically causes my muscles to be extremely weak and to deteriorate as time progresses. Based on other books I've read by people with illnesses of some sort, this is normally the part where they dive into a painfully dull discussion of science and other stupid things that I don't care about. For the sake of my story, all you need to know is that physically, I am superweak, and constantly getting weaker. I have never walked. I've never even crawled. I've been in a wheelchair since I was three years old, and have relied on other people for pretty much every aspect of staying alive since I was born. Are you starting to see how my circumstances might hinder a sense of freedom?

So, how the hell did I end up a thousand miles away from home on an East Coast speaking tour with only my younger brother, two of my best friends, and a camera crew filming me pee? I have no idea. Life has been pretty surreal over the past few years. But when I really think about it, my existence has consisted of nothing but one absurd event after another.

I have always approached the problems in my life with a sense of humor. A big reason this book exists is because of the blog where I started to tell funny stories about my life. That blog, also titled Laughing at My Nightmare, has over half a million followers today. I guess wheelchairs are just "in" right now.

This is the story of life from the seat of my powered wheelchair as it has transpired during the first twenty-one years of my life. I might be dead by the time this book gets published, or I might not be. Either way, I hope for nothing more than to share my story with you and make you laugh.

chapter 1

a "normal" day

The sound of my cats trying to kill each other startles me awake. Oreo and Roxy don't get along very well, probably because Oreo is a prissy prima donna who cares only about herself, and Roxy has an inferiority complex. Every other day, Roxy snaps and attacks Oreo in an attempt to end her existence and become the sole recipient of my mother's love. Their death battles sound like a hurricane smashing through the house. I groan and look at the clock that hangs on the wall next to my bed, 9:45 a.m. Too early. Let them kill each other. I fall back asleep to the soothing sounds of Roxy tearing Oreo to shreds.

> *Fun Fact*
> *I drool so much overnight that I have considered hiring a lifeguard to watch me while I sleep.*

Only forty-five minutes pass until I wake up for a second time. I've never been good at sleeping in. This time, the sun slicing through my bedroom window has stirred me from sleep. I groan again.

"Andrew, can you get me up?" I call. I hear a groan escape his bedroom through his partly opened door. Mom opens it every morning before she and Dad leave for work to make sure he can hear me. I know he heard my call, but it wasn't enough to will him out of bed. I wait for a few minutes, considering how annoyed I'd be in his situation. I call him again.

"Yea, one sec," he calls back, still half asleep. I don't sense annoyance in his voice, and I hardly ever do. He knows I need him.

Andrew groggily enters my bedroom wearing a pair of basketball shorts and no shirt. As per usual, we don't talk much as he helps me get ready. He pulls my blanket off, rolls me onto my back, and after grabbing a pair of shorts from my dresser, gently and meticulously pulls them up my legs and over my butt. The shirt he chose is a little stubborn getting over my left arm, but he gets it on after a few tries and manages not to break any bones.

"Do you need to pee?" he asks.

"No. I'll wait til later," I say.

"Good, because I wasn't going to do it, anyway."

My little brother leans over the bed and slides his arms under my knees and behind my shoulders, lifting and carrying me to my wheelchair. He sits me down gingerly, almost getting me in the perfect position (a nearly impossible task). He unplugs my phone from the charger and sets it on my lap, walks to the kitchen to pour a cup of coffee, which he leaves on the edge of the dining room table for me, then comes back into my room. "I'm going back to bed. Are you good?" he asks. I thank him and drive to the dining room to find the coffee that will inject me with the energy to make it through the day.

This is how Andrew lifts me.

My laptop is sitting next to the cup of steaming coffee (more like coffee-flavored milk, Andrew made it very sweet). Part of Dad's morning routine—after getting me up at 6 a.m. for a shower and putting me back in bed afterward—is to open my laptop on the edge of the table so I have something to do when Andrew goes back to sleep. I can't physically type on a keyboard or lift the cup of coffee to my lips, but like all daily tasks, I've found ways to improvise. I have an app for my iPhone that transforms it into a wireless mouse pad and keyboard (I love you, Apple). Sticking out of my coffee is a superlong bendy straw that I ordered off the Internet. It is long enough so that the straw reaches my mouth when the coffee is sitting on the table. Little adaptations like these are what allow me to thrive.

Oreo walks past me toward her food bowl that sits on the kitchen floor. I am slightly disappointed in Roxy. One of these days she will accomplish her mission, and I will sleep beautifully until lunchtime. I open Netflix and put on an episode of *Breaking Bad* while checking my email and blog. Hundreds of new messages. At this point in my life, the summer of 2012, most of my days start by checking fan mail. Thousands of people from around the world write me to share how my blog has impacted their lives or made them laugh. I am twenty years old, and as my number of followers steadily climbs into the hundreds of thousands, I exist in a constant state of disbelief. The emails will have to wait, though, as will the rest of the work that is starting to pile up for my nonprofit. At that moment I just want to take a break from the insanity and enjoy my coffee while watching Walter White cook crystal meth.

An hour later my phone rings. It's Mom calling from work

as she does every summer morning to make sure Andrew and I haven't set the house on fire.

"Is Andrew awake yet?" she asks.

"Yeah, he's on the couch watching *The Price Is Right*," I lie, not wanting to give her the idea that he's being lazy or irresponsible.

"Whatcha up to?"

"Just watching Netflix."

"What are you guys gonna do for lunch?"

"I don't know. We're fine."

"I know you're fine. I'm just checking. Can't your mom be concerned?"

"Yup, we're good." We say goodbye.

Andrew comes out of his room shortly after. He collapses onto the couch in our living room, and soon, I hear Drew Carey telling contestants to spin the wheel coming from the television. A few minutes later, Andrew yells, "Yo, do you care if Ryan comes over later?" I don't. His friends and my friends inhabit our house most days of the summer, but he still always asks to make sure I don't need his help with anything before inviting people over.

"I just need my teeth brushed, hair combed, face washed, and shoes on," I tell him.

"Yeah, I guarantee that's not happening," he says. Ten minutes later, he helps me do all four things.

Ryan arrives, and Andrew informs me they are going to McDonald's and asks if I want anything. "A McDouble and a

9

large sweet tea," I say. Andrew says, "Okay. So a cheeseburger and a small sweet tea because you weigh thirty pounds, and I'm not wasting money on food you won't eat."

Twenty minutes later, Andrew and Ryan come back with the goods. Andrew cuts my cheeseburger into four quarters and grabs me a plastic fork (metal forks are too heavy for me, but a fork is necessary since I can't lift my hands as high as my mouth). We eat and play FIFA and go swimming. A summer day doesn't get much better in my mind. It's relaxing, simple, and nothing happens to remind me of the disease that's slowly destroying every muscle in my body. Just a normal day in the Burcaw household. I say "normal" but what I really mean is "normal for us." Ever since my diagnosis, the idea of normalcy has taken on a very different meaning for my family and me.

chapter 2

the lazy baby

My life waved goodbye to normalcy in 1992 at the Sayre Childhood Center in Bethlehem, Pennsylvania. I was nine months old, and while the rest of my classmates spent their days crawling around the room, pooping themselves and making a mess of everything they could get their hands on, I was perfectly content to sit wherever I had been placed, playing with whatever toy I had been given, or simply watching my other baby friends explore the world. I never moved. Crawling just didn't interest me.

My observant daycare monitor mentioned my complacent nature to my parents and suggested that they take me to a pediatrician. It was probably "no big deal." Sometimes babies experience delays in physical development, but it was best to play it safe and have a professional check me out. My pediatrician was more concerned. He felt that I needed to be seen by a neurological specialist.

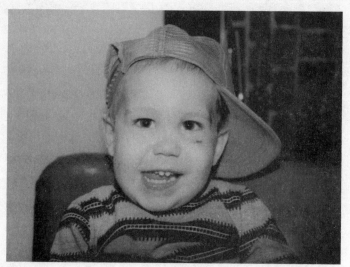
I'm not sure how a sedentary baby winds up with such a grisly scar.

During the neurologist appointment, that "no big deal" became slightly bigger.

After spending an hour watching and interacting with me, the neurologist declared that she was almost certain I had a neuromuscular disease called spinal muscular atrophy (SMA). She couldn't be sure without performing a few significantly more invasive tests, but those needed to be done at a specialized hospital in Philadelphia, so the waiting continued. She warned my parents not to research the disease before I had an official diagnosis; the existing literature would only dishearten (read: scare the shit out of) them.

I need to take a little time to explain the boring facts about my disease. I apologize. If you'd like to make this paragraph more interesting, light your hair on fire and try to finish the paragraph before your scalp starts to melt. SMA is a neuro-muscular disease that affects approximately .0001 percent of the population. (I can't wait for the hate mail that begins: Hey, Fucker, I looked up the prevalence of SMA, and I'll have you know the true percentage is actually .00023 percent." I've learned on my blog that people will get angry and argu-mentative over anything.) The human body has two proteins that help to create and maintain muscle tissue. An individual with SMA lacks one of those proteins, resulting in poor mus-cle development and progressive muscle deterioration over time. Basically my body just didn't feel like developing these proteins while I was in the womb. I was the laziest fetus you'd ever meet.

There are three main types of SMA, aptly named Type I, II, and III. People born with Type I usually die before their second birthday due to severe wasting of lung and heart muscle tissue. On the other hand, Type III individuals usu-ally walk for a few years before their symptoms become ap-parent. Their muscles waste away much more slowly than those of people with the other two types. Type II is really a toss-up. It is characterized as being an unpredictable combi-nation of Types I and III. Important disclaimer: people out-live their prognoses all the time, sometimes by many years. I provide them to give you an idea of the very nature of the disease.

A few months after receiving the unofficial diagnosis from the local neurologist, my parents and I experienced a tiny glimpse of hell as I underwent the necessary tests to confirm the SMA diagnosis at Children's Hospital of Philadelphia. I don't remember it obviously, but I've heard the story from my parents a billion times. One of the tests involved inserting electrified needles into my thighs and shoulders, creating an electric current through baby me. Healthy muscles twitch and spasm when subjected to electricity. In my case, I reacted to the incredible pain with only tears; my muscles remained motionless. As if being electrocuted wasn't enough trauma, the doctors also cut a chunk of muscle from my thigh later that afternoon for another test.

> *Shane Pickup Line: Hey, wanna see my scars? I've got one on my thigh, but you'll have to help me take my pants off to see it.*

The next day my parents were finally given the crushing news they'd been expecting to hear all along. Shane has Spinal Muscular Atrophy Type II.

"Will he ever walk?" asked my father.

To this day, he tells me that hearing the doctor's response was the hardest moment in his entire life.

But therein lies a peculiar detail that defines my family. Finding out about the diagnosis was the most difficult part for them. Accepting it and figuring out how to deal with it came almost naturally.

My parents decided that this diagnosis was not going to cripple the happy life they had imagined for themselves and their son. Life is beautiful, with or without a severely debilitating muscle-wasting disease. Before grief and sorrow even had a chance to sink their teeth in, my parents made a decision. My life would be normal. SMA was not the end, but the beginning. A bump in the road. An obstacle to rise above.

And so, the journey began.

I should mention that everything I know about the process of my diagnosis and early childhood is completely based on the stories my parents have told me. Like everyone else, I have little memory of the first few years of my life. There's a chance that they are lying to me and I do not have SMA. Maybe one of them accidentally dropped me down a flight of stairs as an infant and they decided it would be easier to create this elaborate story than own up to their failures as parents. My entire life could be a hoax. The Illuminati are possibly, if not definitely, involved. (Do you think my book will sell more copies now that I can include Illuminati as a keyword for the Amazon listing?) I will never know.

chapter 3

learning to drive

As a baby I wasn't much different than any other baby. Other than not being able to crawl, I was not limited in any other way. My mom tells me that it was almost nice never having to worry about where I was because I was always exactly where she put me.

I started talking in complete sentences at a very young age, a common trait in SMA Type II–affected individuals. It makes sense. I probably became aware that communication was vital to getting what I needed. If I couldn't reach a toy a few inches away from me, all I needed to do was ask someone and they were more than happy to help. This reliance on others began when I was a baby, and has followed me since.

The real fun began in preschool at the age of three, when I got my first wheelchair. I attended a preschool that specialized in helping the physically and mentally disabled; the only "special" school I've ever attended. It ultimately served me well. There was a physical therapy center within the building, and that is where I learned how to drive.

At first the therapists put me in a small vehicle that looked nothing like a wheelchair. It was basically a box on four wheels. In front of me sat four large arrow buttons, pointing forward, backward, left, and right. I curiously pressed the forward arrow and almost fell over at the unexpected lurch. My eyes lit up as my young mind began to comprehend the independence I suddenly had. Up until this point in my life, movement of any type meant being carried by my parents, or being strapped into the jogging stroller that they used to take me places. I had been conditioned to appreciate my surroundings from wherever I was seated, but now, if I wanted to move left and further inspect the fascinating bug on the wall, all I needed to do was press the left button until I was closer.

This training chair didn't last long. Therapists use it to teach children the basic concept of using a wheelchair to navigate through the world. A few days later, they brought a real wheelchair for me to try. After strapping me securely in place, the therapists explained that instead of directional buttons, I would now use the joystick that sat in front of me to control my movement. This would allow me to have 360 degrees of control of my chair's direction. And, the therapists said, this wheelchair was a lot faster, so I needed to be careful.

Less than twenty seconds later, I had smashed full speed into the padded wall on the opposite side of the therapy room. The therapists gasped. I cracked up laughing.

I was reprimanded for putting myself and other people in

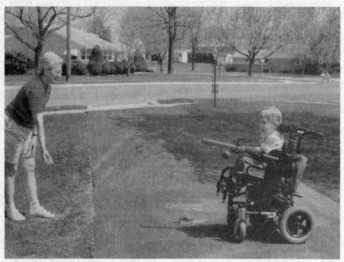

Three months later, I was offered a contract by the Phillies. Nana Jean and I playing baseball in her front yard.

danger. How was hitting a padded wall dangerous? I asked. This question earned me a stern speech on maturity and responsibility, two values I had to learn at a young age. Clearly though, they didn't understand that I was in complete control the entire time. I wanted to hit the wall. In fact, crashing into the padded walls of my preschool became one of my favorite activities. I've always been a bit of a thrill-seeker.

Luckily my parents had a good medical insurance policy that covered the cost of a motorized wheelchair, and the therapists at my preschool were able to convince the insurance company that I needed one for independence at such a young age. I had my own wheelchair a few months later. From that day on, I spent almost every waking hour in the seat of that ridiculously expensive ($28,000) little vehicle.

My family—which now included a little brother named Andrew—and I lived on a quiet street in Bethlehem for the first eight years of my life. Maple Street was lined with towering maple trees that created a tunnel of shade during the summer. Along either side of the road were several town houses. Our home was brick and had a cozy, covered front porch with a baby swing that my dad would push me in to break up the constant wheelchair routine. We didn't have much of a front yard, and the moderately sized backyard was mostly taken up by the winding wooden wheelchair ramp that my dad built so I didn't have to sleep outside. For my brother, our friends, and I, the front sidewalk and back alley became the primary places to play. My enjoyment of wall-smashing quickly turned to sports once my brother was old enough to play them, which was about two days after he began walking.

chapter 4

whoops!

On a humid July day when I was six, instead of racing around outside with my neighbors, I was sitting on the toilet, strapped into my specially adapted backrest, quietly weeping at myself for being so stupid. What was wrong with me? On my bare lap sat our house phone, waiting for me to gather the nerve to call my neighbor, Ben.

A few hours before Ben and I had been spending the day the same way we spent every day of our summer, playing cops and robbers, cowboys and Indians, and other crazy games of our young imaginations. On that particular day we were constructing an epic volcano in Ben's backyard sandbox. By "we" I really mean Ben. Sitting in the sandbox was difficult for me at this point in my life, so I sat above in my wheelchair and played the role of bossy friend who wants to help but can't sit in the sand.

"The left side needs more sand."

"Careful you're gonna wreck it."

"You should try to dig a moat around the outside."

"Oh my God! Move, move, move! I just saw a huge pincher bug by your foot!"

The pincher bug I spotted quickly destroyed our desire to finish the sand volcano, even though Ben's mom was going to allow us to make it erupt with vinegar and baking soda. Instead, we spent the next hour spraying stuff (mostly each other) with Ben's garden hose. It was around this time, after drinking copious amounts of water from the hose, when I noticed that I needed to pee.

In my preschool days, I viewed going to the bathroom as nothing but a nuisance. During the summer, going to the bathroom meant stopping whatever awesome game Ben and I were playing, returning to my house, having my mom carry me upstairs, undressing, using the toilet, redressing, being carried back downstairs, and finding Ben again. The whole process probably took twenty minutes, but that's a lot of time to a six-year-old. For this reason I chose to ignore my bladder on most summer days, holding my urine until it became painful and then some.

The "full bladder pain" became noticeable while we were playing with the hose, but I put it out of my mind when Ben's mom brought out a new Super Soaker to play with. This would be a great weapon to use in our next bank heist.

Half an hour later, as we quietly crept around the back of

A life of crime does terrible things to people. Left to right: Myself, childhood best friend Ben, his brother Harry, my brother Andrew.

the bank that we were robbing (our neighbor's shed) with our fully loaded Super Soaker, I began to sweat and my breathing became rapid and shallow. This was not a nervous reaction to the felony we were committing, but rather my body trying to tell me that I was going to explode if I didn't pee soon. But you don't just go to the bathroom in the middle of stealing one billion dollars from the most highly guarded bank in the entire world.

When the bank guards opened fire with their machine guns, Ben leaped behind a birdbath and fired back at the windows of the shed. It was the climax of the heist. Ben desperately shouted for me to run in for the money while he covered me, but I couldn't pretend anymore. I couldn't even move. A small trickle of urine forced its way out of my body and I lost control.

I closed my eyes and basked in the orgasmic feeling of my painfully swelled bladder emptying. Nothing on earth mattered. Not the fact that I was peeing in my pants. Not the fact that I was doing so three feet away from my best friend. Not the fact that halfway through the emptying I was sitting in a warm puddle. Not the fact that six-year-olds don't pee in their pants. Not the fact that it was running down my legs into my shoes and socks. Not the fact that my mom was going to kill me. Not even the fact that Ben had been shot by the guards and was now lying dead next to me.

"I'll be right back," I said nervously as I finished peeing and started for my house. I didn't think Ben noticed what had just happened, and keeping it that way suddenly became my biggest priority. He'd obviously never treat me the same way if he knew I was a baby that peed his pants. I was entirely convinced that he would associate me peeing in my pants with me being in a wheelchair and he wouldn't want to be my friend anymore.

My mom had reacted exactly how I had expected her to when I arrived home. Lots of yelling about how I needed to learn to stop what I was doing when I had to go to the bathroom. Playing is not more important than taking care of your body, blah, blah, blah.

When she asked if I still needed to go more, I lied and said that I did, making the brilliant reasoning in my six-year-old brain that she would not be as mad if she knew that I had at least been able to somewhat control my bladder. She was. My chair was literally dripping with piss.

After strapping me onto the toilet, she handed me the phone and said, "Call Ben and tell him why you are not allowed back outside today." I stared at her in horror, knowing she had already made up her mind.

I dialed Ben's house number through watery eyes from the seat of the toilet. His number was the only phone number besides our own that I knew by heart, probably from calling it every morning to find out when he could come outside to play. As it rang, I gritted my teeth and tried unsuccessfully to stop my hyperventilating breaths. I hated my mom for making me do this.

Ben's mom answered the phone, "Hello?"

"Hi . . . is Ben there?" I sheepishly asked. I felt like she knew.

"I'll go find him. I thought you guys were outside . . ."

"Hello?" It was Ben.

"Hey, Ben." I started crying again, glancing to make sure my mom wasn't in the bathroom. "Ummm . . . I can't come back out to play."

"Aww, man! Why not?" he moaned.

"Well, I was really, really sweaty when I got inside, and (huff, huff, huff) my underwear and shorts and wheelchair were like wet from the sweat, but my mom thought it was pee so she grounded me. She thinks I peed in my pants," I lied, still extremely embarrassed by the fake story I was telling him.

"Oh . . . darn. Okay, well, can you play tomorrow?"

We did play the next day, but before we tried to rob the bank again, I went back to my house to get ammo and body armor (and to use the bathroom).

Wheelchairs also make great getaway vehicles. Ben riding on the back of my wheelchair.

chapter 5

helplessness is a real bitch

One of my biggest fears has always been not knowing how much longer I have to live. My fear of death is more of a long-term, always-in-the-back-of-my-mind type of fear and usually does not largely affect me on a day-to-day basis. I have another fear, though, and it toys with my mind almost every day, or night, I should say. This fear is completely unjustified, slightly embarrassing, but very real. I am terrified of being stranded in my bed.

I can't do much of anything on my own, including getting in and out of my bed. Every night, someone in my family lifts me out of my wheelchair and puts me in my bed. I am so weak that once I lie down, I rely on other people to move my body and limbs into comfortable positions. Once I am in a sleep-worthy position, usually on my left side, curled up like a baby, the family member that helped me with the transfer turns off my lights and leaves my room. This is when my brain starts to run wild.

If I ever become uncomfortable or need to roll to my other side during the night, I have to yell loud enough to wake someone up so they can come help me. In a typical night, I roll at least one or two times. This reliance on others to stay comfortable is where my fear of being stranded in my bed arose.

> Actual conversation with Andrew:
> Me: Can you pull my socks off?
> Andrew: No. You're just trying to get naked. This isn't Girls Gone Wild, Shane. It's time to go to sleep.

When I was a young kid, say six or seven, there was one single incident I can remember that I believe initiated this whole stupid fear. Our house on Maple Street was a two-story house, which is absolutely the worst living situation for a family with a kid that can't walk. All of the bedrooms were upstairs, so every night, my mom or dad carried me up that flight of stairs to put me to bed. Since I was young, they made me go to bed a lot earlier than they did, so they put me in my bed and then went back downstairs. My parents used a baby monitor well past my baby years; they had to, or else they never would have heard me calling for someone from all the way up in my room. I remember getting anxious between the moment I yelled one of their names and the moment I heard one of them start to climb the staircase. Did they hear me? Should I call again? And I often did call them way more than I needed just to make sure they could still hear me.

Anyway, there was one particular night when my mom put me to bed and told me that she and my dad were going to sit out on the front porch for a little while. My six-year-old brain did not like this because of the distance and walls that would be separating me from their ears, but my mom assured me that they would have the monitor on and that I would be fine. She left my room and about ten minutes later, I decided I needed to call them to make sure they could hear me.

No reply. No footsteps. I called again, louder. Nothing.

Panic started to flood my body and I continued to yell for them. Little did I know the monitor had died and they couldn't hear me at all out on the front porch. I began to cry profusely, all the while screaming for them at the top of my lungs. I was completely certain that something terrible had happened to them, and I was going to be stuck in my bed until I died. For a good forty-five minutes, I tried with all my might to call someone, anyone, for help. When my parents decided to come back inside, they immediately heard me screaming, "HELP ME!" as if I were in serious pain. They ran upstairs and calmed me down, but I was already scarred. The reality that I am absolutely helpless in my bed became burned into my mind.

Even today I can't sleep with my bedroom door closed. If I ever go to bed before my parents, I lie there and worry until I hear them both go to bed. If I know that only one person will be home in the morning, I wake up before everyone else leaves and ask them to put me in my chair so that if something happens to them, I won't be stranded. I have never even taken a nap during the day because I'm afraid that when I wake up nobody will be home and I will be in pain.

My brain tells me that there is nothing to worry about, that my family knows I can't be left alone in bed. But there is always that tiny what-if that ruins everything. What if I wake up in a considerable amount of pain and my dad is at work, my brother is at a friend's house, and my mom falls and hurts herself in the basement?

After experiencing that feeling of total helplessness, it's hard to convince myself that everything will be fine.

chapter 6

shots! shots! shots! shots! shots! shots!

People with SMA eventually die because their bodies suck at fighting off respiratory infections. I'm sure some of them get hit by cars or drown or accidentally overdose on Tylenol, but by and large the leading killer of people with SMA is respiratory infection. Therefore, avoiding respiratory illness is the best way for me to continue being not dead.

One of the biggest causes of respiratory illness in people with SMA is a virus called RSV, which stands for respiratory syncytial virus. According to a random medical encyclopedia I found online, RSV is "a very common virus that leads to mild, coldlike symptoms in adults and older healthy children. It can be more serious in young babies, especially to those in certain high-risk groups. It also hates people that have SMA." I added that last sentence myself.

Since RSV almost always causes a severe respiratory infection in children with SMA, my doctor ordered that I start receiving the preventative RSV immunization at the age of six. From then until fourteen, I received the RSV vaccination every winter. No big deal, right? Well, it would have been no big deal had the shots not been created by Satan himself.

For those seven years of my life, I was forced to get the RSV shot once a month starting in October and ending in March each year. However, the amount of vaccination that had to be injected into me was more than could fit in one needle. In fact, my monthly dosage of RSV immunization had to be divided among four needles. During this period of my life, I received approximately 168 RSV shots. My thighs, where I got the shots because they were the fattest part of my body, used to look like actual pincushions, covered in tiny red needle scars.

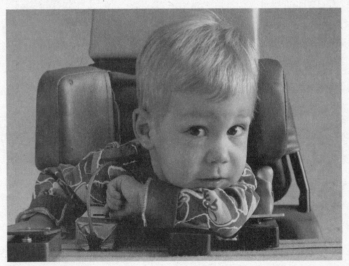

What kind of monster could stick needles into this cutie pie?

With all that being said, 168 shots over seven years is still not that big of a deal. But what made these shots super-extra terrible was that the medicine they had to inject me with was basically the same consistency as chunky beef gravy. Each injection felt like lava as it sloshed into my thigh muscle. The nurse had to push the medicine in at an extremely low rate because it had to go directly into my muscle, and the liquid was so thick that my thigh muscle probably would have fucking exploded if she went any faster. Needless to say, the shots were painful, and I was afraid of them in the worst way possible.

At first, I handled the shots pretty awfully. I would start crying when the nurse walked in with the shots, repetitively scream, "OW! OW! OW!" as she did each one, and I felt no consolation when it was over because I knew I had to do it all again next month. I remember making my mom tell me what day she had scheduled the shots for each month, so that I could mentally prepare myself as the day approached; and by mentally prepare myself I mean freak the fuck out for a week in advance. Eventually she started surprising me on the day of the appointment so that I didn't worry about it before-hand, although I definitely preferred knowing that it was approaching rather than having a great day suddenly ruined by the surprise.

When I was eight or nine, I made a decision to stop crying while I was receiving the shots; I wasn't any less afraid of them, but crying like a baby in front of a pretty nurse started to feel pretty embarrassing, especially when my pants were off to give her better access to my thighs. So one day I expressed this to the nurse and asked if she knew of any secret methods for dealing with the pain of the shots. She told me that it might help if I talked about something else while she was doing it to take my mind off of the pain. Okay, I could try that. She asked me what kinds of things I liked, and I replied football, specifically the Minnesota Vikings, who were my favorite team at the time. We developed a loose plan for me to tell her about the Vikings while she did the first shot.

As the nurse held the needle a few inches above my thigh, she said to start talking, and this is what frantically came out of my mouth:

"Hut 1! Hut 2! Hike! Culpepper drops back and the defense is blitzing! He runs to the ahhhh (shot stabs my thigh) to the left and he is about to get tackled!" As the nurse started pushing the medicine in, the volume of my voice increased significantly and became hysterical, to the point where I was basically screaming, "CULPEPPER THROWS A HAIL MARY TO RANDY MOSS, WHO IS RUNNING DOWN THE SIDELINE! MOSS DIVES AND CATCHES THE BALL WITH ONE HAND! HE STAYED INBOUNDS! TOUCHDOWN!!!"

I can only imagine what other people in the office must have thought when they heard me screaming football commentary at the top of my lungs. Oddly enough, it did help me deal with the pain, and so yelling out narration of random football plays became my method for dealing with RSV shots. I kid you not; I used this same method every month for probably three years.

Eventually, yelling football commentary in the doctor's office started to feel embarrassing as well. Go figure. I also developed a higher pain tolerance around the same time and suddenly RSV shots were not nearly as frightening. Culpepper's miraculous plays were no longer needed to deal with the pain.

I received RSV shots like a big boy for two more years until our insurance company decided to stop paying for them. Their reasoning was that RSV shots are only scientifically proven to be effective on children under the age of two. When we questioned why they had been paying for them for the last seven years, they subtly conceded that they had made a mistake and offered to pay for the shots for one more year.

I've had RSV only once since I stopped receiving the immunizations, and although it resulted in a four-day hospital stay, I was able to fight it off. Knowing that I am unprotected from the risk of RSV almost makes me miss the shots.

Almost.

chapter 7

little baby sauerkraut

I was hospitalized a number of times throughout my childhood for pneumonia. Since my lungs have always been pretty shitty at being lungs, they often had trouble clearing mucus from my airways. Every illness I faced as a child was, in reality, a life-or-death situation. Even today, at twenty-one years old, I'm terrified of going to the hospital because of my unshakable certainty that I will someday die there.

The worst of my early childhood hospitalizations came the winter before my third birthday. This hospital stay was a big moment for a very different reason. One night during my two-week hospitalization, my parents told me that I was soon going to have a baby brother. I was covered in wires and heart monitors, pricked with a painful IV, and barely able to breathe, but suddenly I felt energized and alive. Not even pneumonia could damper my excitement.

"What do you want to name him?" they asked me, forgetting that by this point in my life, sarcasm and humor were already deeply ingrained into my personality.

"Sauerkraut!" I said with a nonchalance that drove both of them into hysterics, earning us some rude glances from other parents of sick children in the large hospital room.

Several months later, I beamed with pride as I held Andrew "Sauerkraut" Burcaw in my arms for the first time. I was immediately more in love with him than my tiny little mind could even comprehend. He was my little brother, and I was going to teach him everything I knew about everything. He was going to be amazing at sports, and I was going to teach him about them. He was going to play video games with me. We were going to be best friends. I was perfectly confident in all of this, and I turned out to be right.

It's a tough call, but I think I'm just a little cuter. Andrew and me.

I searched my brain for an embarrassing fact about Andrew that I could share in my book as a little surprise for him, because as the older brother it's my responsibility to humiliate him in front of thousands of readers when given the opportunity, but I'm having trouble coming up with a story that won't, 1. Land him in jail, or 2. Land me in jail. Some things are better left unsaid.

chapter 8

andrew is a dead man

"How do you remain so positive?"

People ask me this a lot. The origins of my positive nature can be attributed to learning to handle adversity as a young kid. My whole family will tell you that I was always a happy child, constantly looking for the next source of entertainment, never allowing my wheelchair to get in the way of having fun. Still, I'm human and humans get upset sometimes, especially during childhood.

The earliest memory I have of feeling completely devastated and overwhelmed with negative emotions took place when I was probably six or seven years old. One of my favorite things to do as a child was play Nintendo 64. When my best friend and I weren't outside playing cops and robbers, we were sitting in my living room with our minds completely absorbed in a game of Banjo-Kazooie. Can we all just agree that Gruntilda is the worst?

Anyway, if my memory serves me correctly, there was a particular day during the summer when my best friend was away, so I spent most of the day playing Nintendo 64 by myself. I played a bunch of games besides Banjo-Kazooie, such as GoldenEye 007 (which I was never very good at because I couldn't reach the button that was used to fire your gun and that turned out to be a pretty crucial aspect of the game), Mario 64, and Star Wars: Shadows of the Empire (God, I was so lame).

Whatever game I was playing, I remember being totally immersed in the story line when my brother came into the room. Andrew was only three or four at the time, and his favorite thing to do back then was annoy me. Actually, that's still one of his favorite things. I don't remember why, but baby Andrew had a pair of scissors that day, and as soon as he saw how far along in the game I was, he decided it would be funny to pretend to cut the wire that went from the controller to the game console. I screamed at him to stop as he taunted me; I'd never gotten this far in the game and I was fairly confident that if he accidentally snipped the controller wire, it would destroy not only my Nintendo, but also all of the electricity in our house and maybe even the world.

Needless to say I became frantic and enraged as he continued to pretend to cut the wire. Then, in what I still consider to be one of the most traumatic experiences of my life, pretend snipping became REAL snipping in the blink of an eye. Andrew accidentally cut the wire just enough to make the

Nintendo shut off. My unsaved game was gone forever. I instantly lost my mind.

The waterfalls of tears that rapidly ensued were completely uncontrollable, basically involuntary. My life was over. I sat there screaming and crying and screaming and crying until Mom came down from upstairs to see what was wrong. When she walked into the room, I choked back my tears and glared into her eyes as fiercely as I could.

"Andrew is a dead man," was all I said in a confident voice.

Mom apparently didn't understand the gravity of the situation, because her response was laughter. The tears returned when she was obviously much more concerned about Andrew having scissors than the tiny fact that my life was ruined forever.

I spent the next few hours that day crying my eyes out, sulking about the fact that I would probably never be able to get that far in the game ever again. However, at some point, it occurred to me that no matter how much I cried, or how sorry I felt for myself, my game was never going to come back. I realized that I just needed to accept what had happened and move on. I was wasting a beautiful summer day by sitting inside being sad about what happened.

In my life today, I try to approach problems similarly to the way I learned how to handle the Nintendo situation (with less crying, of course). First, I try to assess whether a particular problem warrants getting upset about. To do this, I ask myself a simple question: In ten years, will my life be irreparably and negatively changed because of this problem? If the answer is no, which it usually is, I immediately force myself to stop worrying about the problem. Some examples of problems that fall under this category in my mind include: failing a test, having to do chores around the house, losing any kind of game in sports, breaking up with a girlfriend, getting grounded, falling out of a wheelchair and breaking your femur, etc. The list goes on and on, but the point I'm trying to make to you is that, in my opinion, most everyday problems are not really worth getting upset about.

If, however, I evaluate a problem and decide that it really is a big deal, I move to step two of what I will call my method for dealing with problems. Look at me; I have a method. In my life, most of the problems that fall into this category have to do with my disease. Some examples include: realizing my arms are a lot weaker than they were a year ago, thinking about my long-term future, and being unable to do things because of my wheelchair. These are problems that, no matter how you look at them, just plain old suck—a lot. But therein lies the key to step two of my method. As long as I'm not thinking about these problems, they can't bring me down, so I simply don't think about them! It's not rocket science. There's nothing I can do to solve any of those above-mentioned problems, so what good will come from spending my time being sad about them?

Instead, I focus my mind and energy on doing things that make me happy like laughing, joking, eating, and spending time with friends. The more I think about it, the more I realize that there really is no other way to live.

My method for dealing with problems might not work for everyone, but for me, positivity and happiness are always possible. Always.

My family used to have an old wine bottle with a cork in the top that we called the Crabby Jar. Whenever my brother or I became whiny, as little kids are prone to do, Mom would pull out the Crabby Jar. This jar was magical, because it held all of the Crabbies we had ever put into it. Mom would pull the cork out, we would quickly blow out our Crabbies, and she would quickly jam the cork back so no Crabbies could escape. Once we completed this ritual, there was no physical way to remain angry or sad, since we had literally dispelled the source of those negative emotions into the jar. The underlying idea behind the Crabby Jar is a pretty good indication of the values that my parents stressed. You are in control of your emotions; the choice to be happy is as easy as blowing out your Crabbies.

chapter 9

spine breaking

When I began kindergarten, there was no debate about whether I would be in a normal classroom. I have to thank my parents for not being too protective. Sometimes, parents of children with physical disabilities feel like they need to shelter their kids from the horror of being bullied or the difficulty of functioning in a regular classroom environment. My parents had thus far raised me to understand that my wheelchair did not define me. Sure, my arms and legs didn't work, but my brain, personality, and ability to interact with people were not at all affected. Placing me into normal classes was only natural in their eyes.

Shortly after beginning kindergarten, my teacher suggested that I be tested for advanced placement. This consisted of doing a few mental puzzles that I didn't even realize were the actual test until my parents explained to me later that

I would be starting a once-a-week class for gifted students. It still amazes me that they determined I was gifted just because I knew my colors and shapes pretty well. I think I cheated the system. Or maybe they just felt bad that I was in a wheelchair.

Much of early elementary school is a blur. I made a few friends. I generally enjoyed learning and doing homework. I got excellent report cards, but I hated reading. I can only speak in generalizations about the first few years of elementary school because I just don't remember many specifics. At that time in my life, I began having significant problems with my spine, which culminated in a massive spinal fusion surgery in second grade. Perhaps the intensity of that situation has overshadowed or destroyed the "boring" memories of going to school.

Since my muscles had been slowly deteriorating from the time when I was a little kid, my spine started to curve when I was very young. Basically, the muscles in my trunk, including the muscles that surround my spine, were not strong enough to keep my spine straight. Scoliosis (curvature of the spine) is prevalent among people with my disease.

When it came to scoliosis, my spine was an asshole. Refusing to take its time and gradually curve like most spines affected by scoliosis, my spine wanted to curve as fast as it possibly could. When I went to my yearly checkup at DuPont Hospital in Delaware at the age of six, my doctors were extremely alarmed by how curved my back was becoming. I sat with a ridiculous slouch because I had to compensate for the twisting of my spine in order to hold my head up. When normal people have scoliosis, it's usually only a few degrees of curvature. Here's a picture of me before the surgery. It's tough to see, but notice the Quasimodo protrusion on my back? That's my spine attempting to free itself from my body.

Nothing cures scoliosis like a big bowl of ice cream. Mom, Dad, Andrew, and me.

At that yearly checkup, my doctors calmly explained to my parents that the back brace I had been wearing for a few years was failing about as hard as a back brace can fail. You might notice that the top part of my spine in the picture appears to be intruding on the right lung's personal space zone. My spine was slamming into my right ribcage with as much force as it could muster. The doctors told us that was why I kept getting pneumonia, and that if we didn't do the spinal fusion surgery soon, my lung would collapse, and basically, I would not be alive too much longer after that. The weird thing about my doctors is they never said, "You need to do this or you will die," but even at the age of six, I remember feeling the gravity of their words and understanding I needed the surgery.

Great! So I had the surgery and everything was peachy and that was the end of it!

Nope.

Spinal fusion surgery is the second most dangerous surgical procedure next to brain surgery (If you are a medical professional and would like to dispute this point, kindly send your concerns to 2145 I Don't Care Rd., Idiot, PA 18017), and the doctors made it apparent that there was no guarantee I would thrive after the procedure (read: he might die during the surgery). As you probably know, the spine is a pretty vital part of the human body; it surrounds the precious spinal cord and is surrounded by all of the body's major organs. In a complete spinal fusion surgery, the surgeon cuts the back open from the neck to the tailbone, bends the spine back into a straight line with brute force, and then nails a metal rod to the spine to keep it straight. All in all, the surgery takes eight to nine hours. Sounds fun, right?

The doctors assured us that although there was a big risk, they had done this surgery plenty of times and were confident they could perform it successfully on me. We chose to go through with the surgery; it was scheduled for September. My little mind was completely terrified.

I do not remember much about the day of the surgery because of the shit-ton of anesthesia they gave me. But I do remember lying in a bed watching *Sesame Street* while they started the IV to knock me out and being mad because I was too old for *Sesame Street*.

The surgery went as planned, and I didn't, in fact, die on the operating table. My parents had a little scare when my surgeon walked out into the waiting room about fifteen minutes into the surgery, much too soon for the surgery to be finished. He handed them a cup with one of my teeth in it. Apparently, he had removed it because it was loose and I could have choked on it if the tubes that were shoved down my throat knocked it out.

The earliest thing I remember after the surgery is waking up in a bed and being in a pretty decent amount of pain. I was on my side, and a nurse came in to roll me. I thought I was going to die from the lightning bolts of fire that shot through my back when she moved me even the slightest bit. I didn't want to move ever again. Unfortunately, doctors came into my room shortly after that and coldheartedly told me I needed to poop so they could make sure my intestines were not damaged. I started crying when they explained that a few nurses would lift me onto the toilet. They didn't understand how much pain I was in just lying there, and they wanted to pick me up and put all that pressure on my back? I must have

passed out because I remember them lifting me and screaming at the top of my lungs, but I don't remember sitting on
the toilet or pooping.

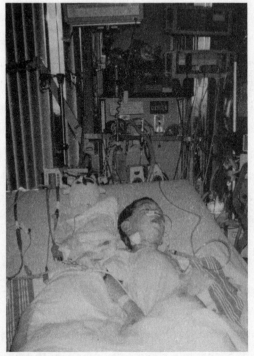

Sexy.

My recovery in the hospital was a three-week process.
Early on I shared a room with a boy who was about my age.
He had been in a severe car accident and his brain was permanently damaged. The nurses told me he had to learn how
to do everything over again—eating, talking, walking—and
that he would never fully recover. This was the first time I
realized I was lucky compared to some people, and although

I didn't fully understand it at the time, I told my dad that I was thankful I only had SMA because it must be so difficult for that kid to relearn how to live.

One day, I was practicing driving my wheelchair down the hospital hallway, (because the surgery had greatly altered the way I sat in my chair) when I passed by a dark, dreary room with a cagelike crib that contained a little boy who was fast asleep among the wires keeping him alive. There were no balloons or people or stuffed animals in this hospital room, which was the complete opposite of my room. I asked one of my nurses and she told me that he was very sick and didn't have any family to visit him or bring him balloons. My room was filled with friends and family and a constantly replenished supply of gift baskets, food, toys, and more balloons than I knew what to do with. This little boy had none of that, but it was the lack of any people in his room that scared me the most. Later that day, I asked my nurse to take some of my balloons and give them to the boy without any family. Even at that naive age, I knew the balloons would not solve his problems, but I hoped that they would at least make him smile.

On the day I was allowed to leave the hospital, I went outside and drove to where my van was parked. When the ramp was unfolded I began to realize something was not right. I drove up the ramp and stopped just before entering the van; my head was too high for me to get in without hitting it on the ceiling. By straightening my spine, the doctors had stretched out my body a solid five inches. I had to ride the entire hour home with my head tipped to the side, which felt just spectacular on my still very sore back.

Clearly I did not give that little boy *all* of my balloons.

Elementary school proceeded normally after my spinal fusion. I was assigned a full-time aide starting in second grade. She was a motherly figure who sat next to me in class and provided physical assistance whenever I needed it. After two years of maturation, I began to realize the negative impact she was having on my social life. My peers didn't want to hang out with Shane and his aide; adults were dumb and they yelled at us for cursing.

Around fourth grade I made my first best friend at school. His name was Eddie, and he quickly made a distinction that many other kids were unable to make; I was separate from my wheelchair and all of its implications. Eddie valued my sense of humor and appreciated that I had to do things a little differently, probably because Eddie was a little different himself.

Eddie was a skateboarder. At a time when other kids were joining baseball and football teams, Eddie spent his time honing his skills on his custom-made Element skateboard. I became obsessively hooked. Skateboarding promoted an alternative, antiestablishment lifestyle. Skaters wore different clothing, thought differently, and most of all, didn't care if the rest of the world thought they were odd. That's exactly what they wanted.

First, I got rid of my aide. The skater mind-set taught me that I didn't need the help of adults; I was supposed to resent it. Eddie sat next to me in every class, so I convinced my parents that he could help me just as well as the aide. Although my motives for favoring the assistance of a close friend were not exactly angelic, it was the beginning of an important and healthy trend in my life; making friendships based on the mutual understanding that I needed physical help and would rely on them for it from time to time.

I also grew my hair out, a staple of the skater lifestyle, and begged my parents to buy my clothes from only the local skate shop. The fact that I couldn't walk never felt like a reason why I couldn't be a skateboarder. When questioned about my style, usually by adults, I simply responded, "If I could walk, I would skateboard. Besides that, I'm a skateboarder in every other way."

I held on to the skater identity for an embarrassingly long time, well past seventh grade.

The worst part is that I made Mom spend at least fifteen minutes making my hair look "perfect" every morning.

chapter 10

a halloween debacle

When I was ten years old, probably in second or third grade, for whatever odd reason, my elementary school was invited to walk in the Bethlehem Halloween parade. I don't really understand why we participated, because it's not like we had a marching band or anything that made us special. Our teacher just told us that we should all dress up as what we wanted to be when we grew up and arrive at the beginning of the parade with our parents on Saturday morning.

Bethlehem is home to approximately 70,000 people, so it's a pretty sizable town. Our yearly Halloween parade is far from a big deal for most people, but I would estimate that a few thousand people line the sidewalks of Main Street to watch it each year. My family had taken my brother and me to watch the parade in years past, with the highlight always being the candy that people in the parade threw to the onlookers. I was excited to be the one with the power to throw candy to whomever I wanted this year.

But first, I had to figure out what I wanted to be when I grew up and how to incorporate this idea into a costume that involved my chair. Costumes that incorporate a wheelchair are a lot more difficult to make than you might think. People always suggest that I should be a car or a tank, and just plop a big painted box over my head and wheelchair, but I've tried this, and the box inevitably slips out of position and falls on top of my joystick, causing my wheelchair to spaz the hell out and crash into groups of young children at top speed. Therefore, most years I have opted to dress up as something that only loosely involves my chair. Here are some examples for you to laugh at:

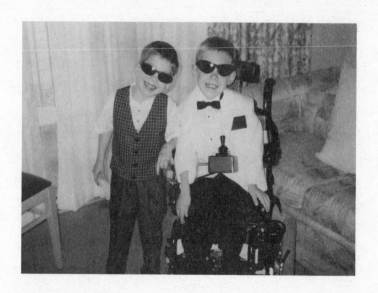

The year of the Halloween parade however, I ended up deciding that I wanted to be a lawn mower (a person who mows lawns, not the physical object) when I grew up. I know, practical. I was only ten, and at the time my dad owned a pretty big lawn business. Since I looked up to him, lawn mower it was. I wish I had a picture of this costume, but I basically dressed in jeans, boots, and a shirt that read, "Burcaw Custom Lawn Service." We attached a wagon to the back of my wheelchair with duct tape and filled it with a bunch of fake lawn-mowing equipment. I looked pretty boss.

Naturally, it was pouring rain the morning of the Halloween parade. Bethlehem's city officials chose to not cancel the parade, and my elementary school made the responsible decision and called everyone to say that we were still expected to be at the parade. Awesome.

It's important to understand that $28,000 electric wheelchairs do not mix well with rain. They are designed to be able to handle a small amount of water, but any prolonged exposure to heavy rain can result in serious damage. Last summer, I got caught outside in a flash rainstorm and my chair didn't work for three days, and as you can probably imagine, being without my wheelchair makes me want to put my head through a wall.

We decided to tough it out and face the rain with everyone else. My dad drove me to the parade; he would be walking next to me along the way because I wasn't old enough to rely on my friends to help me out with stuff yet. Our elementary school was designated as the very last position in the parade. There's nothing like a bunch of little kids in shitty costumes to send a parade out with a bang! This meant that we all had to stand out in the pouring rain while the rest of the parade got started down Main Street.

My father insisted that we cover my chair in a rain poncho while we waited for our turn to join the parade, which in hindsight was definitely a good idea because my chair would have undoubtedly short-circuited and exploded during the hour that we had to stand there and wait.

Luckily, the rain had slowed to a steady mist when it was finally time for us to start moving. My dad took the poncho off and secured the wagon to the back of my wheelchair. Our class merged onto Main Street and started the slow half-mile walk to the end. The couple hundred people who decided to brave the rain to watch the parade acted like my costume was the cutest, most awesome thing they had ever seen in their life. There was a bucket of candy in the wagon behind me, and I instructed my dad to throw handfuls to people, as opposed to single pieces, because when I had watched the parade in past years, I hated all the douchers that threw out only single Tootsie Rolls.

A few blocks down the road, everything was going well, and then out of nowhere, the back right wheel of my wheelchair decided that it had served its duties long enough and broke off from the axle of my chair. All of a sudden, I saw my right wheel rolling down the road in front of me. My chair sharply and immediately veered to the right, and I almost hit my dad, who didn't even notice my wheel had fallen off. He thought I was just driving toward the curb to be funny, so he started to yell at me, but then he must have noticed the empty axle because he ran over and helped me turn my chair off.

The giant street sweeper that cleaned up after the end of the parade was only about 30 feet behind us when this incident took place, so when it passed us, it gobbled up all the tiny pieces that held my wheel in place.

My dad was barely able to guide my chair to the edge of the curb. A few people who were watching the parade and saw the events unfold came over to see if they could help in any way possible. Immediately, my dad became focused on figuring out a way to put my wheel back on—even if was only temporary—because the rain was picking up and I needed to get back to the van where we had left the poncho.

As a joke, my dad asked if anyone had any rope. I will never forget the look on this random dude's face as he reached into his pocket, pulled out a long, thin, rolled-up piece of rope and said, "I do!" (Because carrying rope around in one's pocket is such a normal thing to do.) Anyway, my dad miraculously fashioned some type of knot that held my wheel onto the axle long enough for me to make it back to the van.

All in all it could have been a lot worse; the street sweeper could have eaten me alive, or I could have been walking in the parade on my own, or I could have crashed into an old woman and killed her, so I guess I can't complain about how terrible that Halloween parade really was.

chapter 11

slam dunk

When I was in third grade, my family moved to a new house in a neighborhood not too far from the one in which I spent the beginning of my life. That summer, Andrew and I met our new next-door neighbor, Pat, who was a year younger than me and would eventually grow up to be one of my closest friends.

We spent most summer days trying to find ways to stay cool, which usually amounted to spraying ourselves in the face with the hose, since neither of our families had a pool. When we weren't doing that, we could be found shooting hoops in Pat's backyard.

Pat's house had a wraparound driveway, which created a large paved area in the back that was great for all types of sports. Pat's family had recently installed a superlegit, glass-backboard basketball hoop that made us feel like we were

Pat's usual attire.

training to someday play in the NBA. I can't shoot a basket-ball, so I would usually just play defense and try to demolish my brother's shins whenever he tried to shoot. I also set picks (blocked) like a monster. I once almost killed a kid at recess when he blindly ran full speed into one of my immovable wheelchair picks, but I digress (I love saying that).

There was one particular day when one of us threw out the idea that it would be awesome if we could dunk. Of course that would be awesome; dunking was the coolest thing ever back in those days. Too bad that superlegit basket was also super-too-high for us children to reach. We even tried using a mini-workout trampoline to dunk, but we were just too young and short. By "we," I mean them, I was just too much in a wheelchair to dunk.

I am admittedly a very stubborn individual at times; when I get an idea in my head, I can be extremely annoying/pushy/relentless until I accomplish whatever I am trying to get done. This was one of those times. I knew there had to be a way to help my friends dunk. Before telling them my idea, I told Pat to go grab the long rope his parents kept upstairs in case they ever had to climb out a window during a fire. Don't ask. Whether it's a good or a bad trait, I am also pretty good at manipulating people; not in an evil way, just in the kind of way that I knew once Pat went through the work of acquiring the rope, he would be less likely not to allow me to at least try my idea.

Once he had the rope, I explained that our parents might not like what we were going to do, but none of them were home and it wouldn't take long, so everything would be fine. My idea was to tie a noose on one end of the rope for my brother to lie in, loop the rope up over the basketball hoop, and attach the other end to my wheelchair. I would drive in reverse, which would pull my brother up to the height of the rim so he could chill there while we threw him alley-oops. It was perfect, and nothing could go wrong.

Andrew and Pat surprisingly agreed, and we started setting up the system. On our first attempt, as I slammed my chair into reverse, my brother shrieked in pain and I quickly let him down before he was a foot off the ground. The rough rope on his bare skin (he had his shirt off because it was hot), in addition to his entire body weight being supported by a rope going across his stomach, apparently hurt pretty bad. I told Pat to go grab a couch pillow.

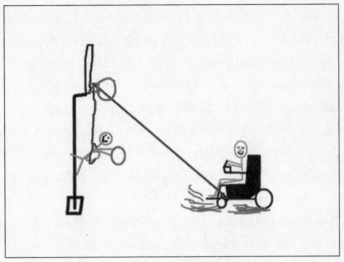

Dramatic reenactment. Oh, did I mention I'm also an artist?

The next try, with the couch pillow between the rope and my brother's body, worked much better, and to all of our amazement, he started lifting off the ground toward the basket. Then we had a problem. My wheelchair ran out of strength to keep lifting him, and despite being in full reverse, neither of us were moving. Pat ran over, grabbed the rope, and pulled with me; slowly my brother inched higher. As he neared the top of the basket, he became significantly heavier, which is probably some kind of physics problem, but I don't understand it. My tires started spinning and we lost a little ground. For a good five minutes we battled gravity in this manner, while my brother bobbed up and down like something that bobs up and down.

All of a sudden I heard someone scream, "WHAT ARE YOU GUYS DOING?" It was my dad, and to my relief he was laughing. He walked over, saw us struggling to keep my brother in the air, and said that probably wasn't very good for my chair. Defeated, we lowered my brother back down and begrudgingly untied both ends of the rope.

Then I had an even bigger problem. I noticed my wheelchair now only turned left; I couldn't drive in a straight line or turn right at all. My dad noticed, too, and came over to see if the rope had knocked something out of whack.

It turned out that our little stunt had completely destroyed both my rear gear motors, which had to be replaced at the price of $4,000 each. Whoops.

chapter 12

daydreaming

When I was young, I went through an odd phase where I constantly had these intensely detailed daydreams about having a paintball fight inside my elementary school. I've never held a paintball gun. In fact, I don't think I've ever even been with someone who's had a paintball gun. Water guns were as far as my parents ever let us get in that realm of entertainment.

The most experience I've had with guns was that Pat's older brother had a BB gun that was occasionally brought out while I was at their house. His brother was in high school and fully aware of the incredible control he had over us with that gun in his hands. He only ever shot Pat, but the howls of pain that escaped Pat's mouth when he did made me flinch whenever the gun's barrel swung in my direction. We simply had to bow down and concede whatever his brother wanted once the gun came out.

Here's how the scenario usually went:

Brother: I'm playing video games now.
Pat: NO. We're playing. Mom said we could.
Brother: [gets gun] I'm playing video games now.
Pat: You're playing video games now. We love you.

My experience with paintball guns was even further limited. I once found an unpopped paintball near my house and thought it was cool, a little secret squishy treasure. I asked my brother to hand me the unknown object and began massaging it between my fingers because the soft sack of mystery felt amazing.

It popped, scaring the shit out of me, and covering my lap and wheelchair in red paint. My mom was thrilled.

Anyway, my daydreams about massive paintball fights seem kind of weird now, given my aversion to guns as a child. The daydreams usually took place when I was trying to fall asleep. Does that still count as a daydream? I don't care. They began with team selections. In my head I'd see a never-ending row of everyone I knew, or at least the people I liked. There were always two teams: my team and the other team that consisted of everyone I didn't pick for my team. I'd go down the line of potential assassins and weigh the pros and cons of having him or her on my team. Pat's older brother was always a given. He was fast and tall and a great shot, at least in the close quarters environment of Pat's living room, where I'd seen him perform. My dad, hmmm, probably not. His strength and protective nature were definite selling points, but I didn't think he'd be able to swiftly and silently navigate the halls of my school where the battle royal was taking place. There was no way in hell he'd be able to perform a diving-across-the-hallway-while-firing-his-gun maneuver without getting hurt, even in my land of make believe.

Teams were picked and the fight would begin with my team and me huddled at one end of the school. I was in charge and whispered directions to them about who would be traveling together and what our methods of attack would be. "Stay inside the alcoves in the walls. Diving is the best way to avoid being hit." I was obsessed with diving.

Oh, I guess it's important to mention that I wasn't in a wheelchair in these daydreams. Wheelchairs aren't exactly stealthy, and back then I was able-bodied in all of my dreams.

The most vivid part of my fantasies started when I set off down the dark hallway toward the other team. After handing out orders to my teammates, I always took off on my own. (There's probably a deep-seated, psychological reason for this fact.) Where the dream had previously been from a third-person point of view, it now switched to first person. I became myself traveling through the building, constantly checking my paintball cartridge to make sure I had enough ammo, scanning the hallway for enemies, ducking into alcoves, diving all over the place for no reason. When I did come across a member of the other team, we inevitably entered into a dramatic standoff, both of us pressed into the safety of an alcove, peeking out every so often, firing off erratic paintballs toward the other, more diving across the hall for no reason. I always won. My team of fighters never reentered the daydream. Instead, I'd clear out the building by myself, and either fall asleep celebrating my victory or snap out of my dream to imagine the awesomeness of being able to someday dive through the hallways of my school playing paintball with my friends if my disease was ever cured. Since I wasn't confined by my wheelchair in the dream, the possibilities for entertainment were endless.

young love

My first serious crush occurred in fifth grade.
This was the age when most of my friends began to pair off,
or at least that's what I understood from all the rumors that
floated around the cafeteria during lunchtime. *Did you hear
that Joey touched Megan's butt during gym class? Ryan went to
Cassie's house last night and her parents caught them making
out! Did you see the used condom by the monkey bars? Brian
claims it's his!*

Everyone starts to get a little horny in fifth grade, and I
was no exception. At this point, I still had no conception of
dating and relationships. Many of my friends were girls. I often
hung out with them outside of school. We played video games
and walked (I rolled) to 7-11 for Slurpees. Innocent stuff.
Then, around the same time all of the fifth grade boys were
gathered into a room and told about erections by the gym

teacher, a switch went off inside me. Suddenly the weird changes occurring in my body made sense. Morning wood was not just a random act of nature designed to make life embarrassing when my dad woke me up and helped me get dressed for the day; it was a sign that I was old enough to have a girlfriend (which, honestly, did not make the situation with my father any less embarrassing).

Upon having this realization, I simultaneously began feeling like I was a little late to the party. All of my friends either had a boyfriend or girlfriend or plenty of stories about things they had done when their parents were not around. Many of their tales were probably fabricated—looking back, I have trouble believing that any of my eleven-year-old friends had actually lost their virginity—but in the moment, I believed them and thus felt like I was being left behind. Girls didn't want to come play video games and drink Slurpees anymore. After all, what would their boyfriends think? I needed a girl-friend, or I risked becoming a "loser."

One of my closest female friends at the time, Jenny, be-came the target of Operation Fifth Grade Hormones. It was generally accepted among the boys that Jenny was the hot-test girl in elementary school. Her boobs were winning the developmental race by a long shot, and she was athletic, a quality of high value at that age. She was sassy, but in a cute way that gave meaning to the multitudes of awkward erec-tions experienced by the fifth grade male population. At recess one day, she kicked a friend of mine square in the balls for making fun of her. It was the best moment of his life.

Jenny and I connected in the classroom more than anywhere else. She was kind and funny and always willing to help me, but in a way that felt like we were just close friends.

She came over to my house several times. She and my brother played tackle football in our front yard, then we ate some ice cream and did homework. Clearly, I had no reason to think she was into me. But that wasn't going to stop me.

I knew from everything my friends had told me that I needed to "ask her out" if I wanted her to be my girlfriend. That scared me shitless. If you've ever read the poem "The Lovesong of J. Alfred Prufrock," by T. S. Eliot, he perfectly describes the neurotic internal debate I felt while working up the nerve to ask Jenny out. If you haven't read it, please mark your page here and go do so now. You can always come back to this, and if I'm being honest, Eliot's poem is way better than this book. In fact, you should probably just throw this book away and go buy some of Eliot's work. (Just kidding, don't do that, please.)

Anyway, I've always been a very analytical person, to the point that it occasionally crippled me more than my disease could. If I asked Jenny to be my girlfriend, and she said yes, it would be the greatest accomplishment of my life. I would have a girlfriend. Kids in wheelchairs don't get girlfriends very easily. This would be a big step in proving to the world that I was different. On the other hand, she could say no.

Everyone knows that you can't ever go back to being "just friends" after a failed proposal. Not to mention the overwhelming embarrassment of being denied and the implication that it meant I wasn't good enough to have a girlfriend, which in my mind would obviously be because of my wheelchair. In a way, it felt like asking Jenny out would dictate my experience with females for the rest of my life.

I had two options. Risk failure by asking her out and maybe just maybe she would say yes, or simply not even try and avoid facing the probable reality that girls would never want to date me. After some serious mental deliberating, I decided to go for it.

I called out to her as she came down the slide the next day at recess, interrupting her game of tag. She walked over, sweating and panting, and asked what was up. Before I could answer, someone ran up behind her and slapped her on the back.

"TAG! JENNY IS IT!" the little twerp screamed. Jenny rolled her eyes and ignored him, but I couldn't help feeling like my proposal was already off to a terrible start.

"Hey, Jenny I know this might be weird, but would you want to go out with me? I really like you." Boom. No beating around the bush, no small talk, just a giant question, presented with as much confidence as a fifth grade boy could have.

No hesitation on her part, "I like you a lot, too, but I just want to be friends!" she said, before smiling like an actual princess, then turning around and sprinting back to her game of tag.

My ego apparently refused to accept that answer, because instead of sulking away to cry behind the giant oak tree, I followed her.

"Jenny, wait!" I yelled. "Seriously, I really like you!"

She paused her game again to give me the same answer as before. My mind didn't understand. Boys I knew had no trouble getting girls to go out with them. In fact, many of my guy friends had been asked out by girls. There had to be a reason why she only wanted to be friends. Deep down I knew the reason, but again, my stupid fifth grade self didn't feel like facing this reality, so I continued to follow her throughout the playground.

"Why?" I asked her when I was close enough for her to hear me. No response. I asked again, this time yelling to her as she swung across the monkey bars. Still no answer. For the rest of our twenty-minute recess period, I continued to follow her like a lunatic around the playground, accosting her whenever I got close enough.

Jenny and I never dated.

However, there was a brief period later in fifth grade when I hung out with the same girl at recess for a few days in a row. She shared her lollipop with me once and I thought things were getting pretty serious; I woke up the next morning with strep throat and that was pretty much the end of that. It wasn't until two years later when this same girl told me she had considered us to be "together" during those few days that I realized she was my first girlfriend. Romantic, I know.

My new pickup line: Hey, do you want to make out with me? You do?! Great! I'm just going to need you to fill out this quick medical questionnaire. Have you experienced any coughing, wheezing, sore throat, watery eyes, headaches, stomach pains, runny nose, or fevers within the last week? I'm sorry, I just really can't afford to get sick.

chapter 14

middle school madness

The end of fifth grade meant the end of elementary school and a transition into a much larger middle school. The middle school you attended was determined by the location of your house, which led to the reluctant severing of many friendships (except for the kids with parents who provided false addresses to send their bratty children to whichever middle school they wanted). Middle school means many different things depending on where you live, but in Bethlehem and surrounding areas, it refers to grades six through eight, which meant I had to reassume my position at the bottom of the totem pole. The adults in my life teased me that middle school was a big, scary place from hell, but during my first week of sixth grade, I was alarmed to discover that they kind of weren't teasing after all. Middle school was terrifying.

Everything was so different than what I had grown accustomed to. In middle school, a bell rang at the end of class, causing an avalanche of students in the hallway as everyone raced to their next class before the late bell rang. The days of walking in single file lines, led by a "Line Leader," were long gone. In elementary school, when the teacher said, "marshmallows in your mouth," everyone had to pretend their mouths were full of marshmallows and got completely silent. In middle school, no one followed the "marshmallows in your mouth" rule anymore. Let's be honest, the hallways of East Hills Middle School were not an avalanche; they were a chaotic clusterfuck. Decency was thrown out the window and replaced with screaming, running, shoving, book-bag throwing, cologne abusing, and making out against lockers. I cautiously made my way through this chaos for the first few days of classes, but eventually even I lost my humanity in this zoo. Being the nice guy just didn't work here. Patiently waiting for people to get out of my way in the hallway became old very quickly, and I started navigating my chair through the crowd with less regard for the lives of others. Many shins were permanently damaged at the hand of my merciless driving.

Another difference in middle school was that every student was given a spiral-bound homework calendar at the beginning of the year. Whether you wrote down your assignments was completely up to you. Only a year ago, I had been required to get a parent's signature on a weekly homework calendar every night. This new freedom, mixed with my lazy but confident personality, led me to use my homework calendar a grand total of zero times, convincing myself that I could keep all of my assignments organized in my brain. Turns out I couldn't, which I was forced to accept when I got an unbelievably crushing B on my first report card; it was in social studies, though, so in hindsight, who cares? I didn't do the logical thing and change my ways to become a more organized and responsible person, but rather settled into a lifelong routine of half-assing school because I didn't feel like putting in the effort to stay organized.

Middle school also presented the obstacle of making new friends, which scared me. Several of my closest friends from elementary school attended the same middle school, alleviating some of my stress, but I knew I wasn't going to get through life with the same group of three or four people. Branching out felt like a step that everyone had to make at some point, but for me, meeting new people meant having more people who I could rely on to help me. Therefore, making friends was vitally important to my ability to function in society. Anything that is vitally important to survival will inevitably be stressful.

When you look like I do—a starving Ethiopian child with a balloon head who basically drives a robot—making new friends can feel daunting.

Here's the scenario that I feared most: I'd enter new classes and be seated next to kids I didn't know. They would feel awkward about sitting next to the kid in the wheelchair and would subsequently not want to become friends. Sure, I had no doubt that they would be decent enough to help me with things that I asked for, but that's where our interaction would end. I would spend every day going to school, being lonely, and not talking to anyone. I would turn into a "loser" who had no friends. People would permanently view me as different and unapproachable because of my disease.

Maybe in a way, my fear of not making friends is a universal one. However, in my mind, my wheelchair and disease would be the unfair cause of never making friends.

To combat the possibility of this imagined scenario ever becoming a reality, I spent a considerable amount of time obsessing about the way kids would perceive me when middle school started. I bought cool clothing, thinking that if I wore the same clothes as them, they'd have an easier time seeing me as their equal. I continued to let my hair grow, since being rebellious and having long hair would obviously be a sign to people that I was normal. I ran through potential conversations in my mind and practiced asking for help in cool ways that didn't sound pathetic and annoying.

Middle school taught me a lot about meeting new people, which inspired this list.

Things NOT to do when meeting someone in a wheelchair for the first time:

1. Spit on them
2. Tell them how great it is for them to be out in public
3. Hit them

4. Rustle their hair affectionately

5. Kick them

6. Throw them out of their wheelchairs

7. Push them down a flight of stairs

8. Call them "Buddy"

9. Steal their money

10. Challenge them to a foot race

Then middle school started. Sure enough, in my first class of the first day I was assigned a seat next to someone I didn't know, a pretty girl who was definitely one of the popular girls at her elementary school. Upon realizing she had been assigned a seat next to wheelchair kid, the facial expression that she tried to secretly flash to her friends told me I had already been labeled as weird. My palms doubled their output of sweat. We sat next to each other in silence, as I discovered I was not nearly as brave and socially skilled as I had convinced myself to be in the weeks leading up to this moment. Say something you idiot.

"Hi, I'm Shane," I said, my voice probably noticeably shaking.

"Hey, Shane, I'm Samantha. Do you like East Hills?"

That was an odd question for a pretty girl to ask. And she asked it with a clear condescending tone in her voice, like she was speaking to a toddler. She already thought I was mentally challenged.

"Yeah, it's pretty cool, but the hallways are so fucking crowded! I accidentally ran over like four people on the way to class." Cursing was an excellent way to show social normalcy. She noticed. Her giggle was nervous but genuine, like she wasn't sure if I was being funny on purpose. I continued, "Hey, could you possibly be my helper for this class? I just need help with small stuff like getting my books out of my book bag. I would do it myself, but I'd probably end up on the floor." She laughed, a little harder this time. There's nothing like meeting someone who quickly understands my sense of humor. I watched her facial expressions and heard her voice completely shift over the next few minutes as she began to realize I was a normal kid. My sense of humor allowed her to see past my wheelchair. Getting people to see past my wheelchair was my one of my biggest concerns when I was young. This desire came from not only my interactions at school, but also a particular event during a summer camp for disabled kids that made me question how nondisabled people perceived me.

Please don't attempt to shake my hand. I know it's tempting; my severely atrophied arms are really sexy, but literally the only possible outcome of trying to shake my hand is an extremely awkward situation. I will chuckle and say something like, "I...uh...can't really...uhh..." and you will realize that I can't even extend my arm, let alone shake back, forcing you to pretend that you had meant to pat me on the head all along, like I'm a cute little wheelchair puppy.

You will probably assume that I didn't notice your creative, on-the-fly problem solving. After all, people in wheelchairs have no social skills. But I did notice, and now all I can think about is how ridiculous it would be if you introduced yourself to everyone by patting their heads.

Please consider utilizing fist bumps or tiny kisses on the cheek to greet me. I prefer a little tongue, but I won't be picky.

chapter 15

cripple camp

The summer before middle school, I attended a weeklong summer camp for kids with muscular dystrophy run by the Muscular Dystrophy Association, which has helped my family tremendously throughout my life. (There are over forty types of muscular dystrophy, diseases that involve muscle deterioration in one way or another. My disease, SMA, falls under that umbrella.) Camp is one of the MDA's biggest programs, taking place all across the country every year, allowing thousands of kids with MD to spend a week away from their parents doing things like swimming, boating, fishing, and tons of other stuff that disabled kids might not get to do too often. When my parents asked if I'd like to go, I was enticed by being away from them for a whole week. Sure, I'd be assigned a full-time counselor whose job was to keep me alive for the week, but living without them still felt like a step toward independence. However, at that age, nothing made me more uncomfortable than being surrounded by other people in wheelchairs. I desperately wanted to show the world that I was normal despite my disability. Looking back, I think this frame of mind was further solidified by my week at summer camp.

There was another kid at this camp who had the same exact disease as me; we shall call him Tim. I'm going to try my best to be as honest and fair as I can when I describe Tim, but you have to understand, during this week of camp, Tim was my archfuckingnemesis. I hated Tim. Today, I realize I probably didn't give him enough of a chance, and my opinion of him was shaped by my thirteen-year-old mind, so there is a good chance that Tim is actually a very cool dude (doubt it). However, this was certainly not the case back then. We'll get to Tim in a little bit.

When I arrived on the first day of camp, the first thing I noticed was that all of the other kids were, or acted, younger than me, which instantly gave me second thoughts about letting my parents leave me there for a whole week. I could smell immaturity in the air. While my parents got me signed in with the camp officials, a bunch of wheelchaired kids chased each other around, wielding balloon swords. A few of them were young enough that balloon-sword fighting was an acceptable and normal thing to be doing. However, a couple of them were at least as old as me, if not older, and it bewildered me how they were getting such a huge kick out of

PRETENDING to stab other kids with their balloon swords. I remember wanting to scream at them, "It's a balloon! It won't hurt if you stab each other! What are you guys even doing?" I immediately disliked every kid at the camp.

Another observation I made in the first few minutes of arriving was that almost none of these kids had shoes on. Some had only socks; most just let their bare feet flop around in the breeze. All of them had severely atrophied ankles like me, but I wore splints that held my feet straight during the day and over my splints I wore normal shoes. I wore shoes because I often went out in public, where wearing shoes is the socially acceptable behavior. Additionally, I was well aware that my atrophied feet look weird to other people. Gross, atrophied feet hanging out for everyone to see were just another reason for people to be hesitant about engaging me as a normal human being. I started to feel extremely uneasy as it dawned on me that none of these kids understood this concept. My young mind started racing. This meant that these kids probably didn't have too many friends, which meant they probably didn't understand how to have normal human interactions, which was why they were all acting so immature! It all clicked in my mind. Look, I feel completely fucked up for thinking this way and for judging all of them so quickly, but if I'm going to be 100 percent honest with all of you, I have to admit that my judgments were actually pretty accurate, which blew.

Am I saying that if you're in a wheelchair and you don't

wear shoes, you are an immature social outcast? No, of course not. Unfortunately, the kids at this camp ingrained in my mind the idea that physical appearance has a big effect on how others treat me. I hate to say it, but these kids made me understand how easy it is to look at someone in a wheelchair and write him off as socially awkward because he just doesn't look normal.

Anyway, after my parents checked me in, it was time to take my luggage to my cabin, and to meet my personal counselor who would be playing the role of caregiver during the upcoming week. I was unbelievably fortunate in that my counselor was the chillest dude ever; he genuinely treated me like I was just one of his friends, which made saying goodbye to my parents a lot easier. Once we got settled and all the parents had gone home, I began talking to the other kids and counselors in my cabin. This is when I first met Tim.

Tim was probably sixteen-ish, making him one of the oldest kids at the camp, and a few years older than me. I could tell right away that Tim thought he was God's gift to the camp. He told jokes that weren't funny and stories that were obviously not true; the other kids completely bought his bullshit, and Tim loved that kind of attention. The best way I can describe Tim for you is that his favorite band was Limp Bizkit.

We all went outside, and Tim felt it was necessary to show everyone how fast his wheelchair was. Cool Tim, my chair is fast, too. Nobody cares. The most annoying part was that

Tim was pretty popular among the counselors, but in the fakest way possible. They had to give him attention; he was constantly trying to impress them, and nobody was going to deny Tim the attention he demanded, after all, he's in a wheelchair.

The fact that Tim had the same disease as me was really what made me hate him. I felt like I knew him better than anyone at the camp. I knew his SMA did not affect his brain and social skills, so why was he acting like such a tool? A tiny voice in the back of my mind kept saying, "You're not so different from Tim yourself."

It was so completely obvious to me when the counselors pretended to laugh at his jokes and pretended to believe his stories. Tim seemed totally oblivious to all of this, which made me nervous. Was I misinterpreting the counselors' interactions with me as being genuine, when in reality they were really just humoring me the same way they humored Tim? Up until this point in my life, I felt like I was pretty good at reading people's faces and their tone of voice to determine whether they were genuinely interacting with me, or if it was the fake "you're in a wheelchair, so I'm being nice to you" type of interaction. Tim made me severely doubt myself.

On one of the first days of camp, our cabin went to the swimming pool for the afternoon. This meant that all the counselors had to carry their respective camper into the pool so we could "swim." Tim immediately started telling anyone that would listen about how long he could hold his breath.

I remember asking my counselor to carry me to another part of the pool where Tim wouldn't annoy us. Tim continued telling everyone about how he was a master underwater swimmer or some bullshit like that even though his counselor wasn't allowing Tim to show off his skill for fear that Tim would drown.

Later on, a female counselor I had become friends with was holding me in the water and she dared me to challenge Tim to an underwater breath-holding contest. I talked to my counselor about it, and he was cool with it as long as I promised to tap his arm when I needed to come up for air.

So we made our way over to Tim and his counselor, and I casually asked Tim if he wanted to see who could hold their breath longer underwater. In retrospect, I have absolutely no idea why Tim accepted this challenge, but he did.

Ready, set, go! Both of our counselors plunged us under the water to start the contest. At this point, had there been any onlookers unfamiliar with what was taking place, they probably would have called 911 to report two heinous individuals drowning disabled kids in a pool.

I'll have you know, I'm actually a highly adept deep sea diver.

I kid you not, within five seconds I noticed Tim start to freak out underwater. His counselor must have noticed, too, because he pulled Tim up for air right away. I was going to stay under as long as possible just to make him feel stupid for being such a dick about holding his breath. All of a sudden, from under the water I noticed people scrambling out of the pool. There was obviously something going on, so I tapped my counselor's arm to come up for air. When he brought me up, I was completely horrified, yet slightly amused. Tim had thrown up in the pool and was continuing to throw up all over himself as the counselors made a huge deal out of getting him out of the water. This was all too perfect. The vomit started spreading around the pool and everyone was disgusted beyond belief. The camp officials had to cancel swimming for the rest of the day, which upset everyone.

Real smooth, Tim.

Today, I feel pretty awful for hating Tim so much. He was just being himself, and I was too insecure to deal with it. However, this incident in the pool left me with the belief that I was never going to get along with other people in wheelchairs.

Luckily for me, the counselors at the camp soon realized I was slightly different from most of the other kids. We joked around and talked about things that I doubt they discussed with the other campers. On the last night of camp, the counselors let me stay up all night with them, just chilling and eating pizza while the other kids slept. For my thirteen-year-old mind, that was a pretty awesome experience, and it taught me that I had the ability and social skills to make genuine friends in a situation where they could have just been "pretend nice" to me because I was in a wheelchair.

chapter 16

the dance

Because camp took place the summer before sixth grade, it probably served as a confidence booster when interacting with new people like the hot girl who sat next to me that you read about earlier. As the school year progressed and spring approached, the infamous sixth grade dance became the hot topic of discussion. By this point I had settled in with a group of friends who teetered on the border of the "popular" crowd and the not-quite-as-popular-but-still-sociable-and-genuinely-funny crowd. One of those friends was my cousin Rebecca. Becca is my dad's brother's daughter, and even though we are the same age and only live a few blocks from each other, we didn't see each other very often until middle school. She went to a different elementary school and was involved in sports because she was about 900 feet tall by the age of ten. Her parents are divorced, so our families only saw each other several times a year. We got together for holidays and occasionally on birthdays, but for whatever reason, Becca and I kept our distance at these family gatherings. Maybe she was afraid of my wheelchair, or perhaps I smelled bad. Whatever the reason, we just didn't interact when our families got together. In fifth grade, I couldn't tell you much more than Becca's name, age, and that she was good at basketball. Then we had some classes together in sixth grade and discovered that we both found incredible pleasure in making fun of each other.

Becca and me. Apparently all Burcaws got the "extremely good-looking" gene.

Becca didn't give two shits that I was in a wheelchair unless she could somehow use my disability to further insult me. Making fun of one another was the crux of our beautiful relationship. I asked her to close her mouth during lunch because her teeth made me gag. She asked if I needed my diaper changed in front of pretty girls.

Our conversation went something like this:

"Becca, can you get my laptop out of my book bag?"

"Can you stop being helpless and get it yourself?" she said.

"Can you brush your teeth for once?"

"Can you even brush your own teeth?"

Basically if you were to listen to a conversation between Becca and me, you might get the sense that we hated each other, but we understood that the constant insults hurled back and forth were not meant to be serious.

Anyway, as the sixth grade dance grew closer, all of my friends started to get very excited. For the few weeks leading up to the dance, our lunchtime conversations went like this:

"Did you hear that Ben asked Laura to the dance?"

"Did she say yes?"

"I don't know. Laura was supposedly going with Chase, but then they got in a fight because he told Kaity that she was hot."

"Oh my God! Seriously?"

"Who are you guys going with?" one of my friends would inevitably ask the rest of the table.

"Emily."

"Hannah."

"Obviously Taylor since we've been dating for three weeks."

I sat quietly munching on my burrito, laughing when appropriate, joking when it felt right, but generally not contributing much to the conversation. My friends never questioned me about who I was taking to the dance. They all seemed to know I wasn't taking anyone. I planned on attending, but I was confident that no girl would want to go with me, so I didn't even bother going through the motions of getting my hopes up only to be rejected. Flying solo wasn't the end of the world. Some of my friends were doing the same thing, including Becca, who could have taken any boy she wanted, but felt that the whole concept was rather silly. She and I decided to just go together, since we had the same group of friends, anyway.

The night of the big dance finally arrived. Sweat had penetrated through the quadruple layers of Old Spice and was creating a tiny river down the side of my body, and I hadn't even left yet. I may have been attending the sixth grade dance with a member of my own family, but that didn't stop my mind from hyping this night up as a huge milestone in my quest for normalcy and acceptance. Not having a girlfriend to attend the dance with felt lame, but Becca and I would have an amazingly hilarious night despite that fact. Also, in the back of my mind, I held on to the hope of catching a pretty girl's heart on the dance floor. I needed to be on top of my game.

I had to start by looking fresh. My dad knew how big this night was and didn't complain as I asked him to shower me, change my outfit several times, brush my teeth, help me do mouthwash and reapply deodorant, and comb my still-very-long hair multiple times. It took us over an hour, which was an eternity compared to our normal routine of carelessly-grab-shirt-and-pants-that-probably-don't-match-and-only-partake-in-personal-hygiene-if-absolutely-required. My dad was a champ for putting up with me. As much as I tried, nothing that I did made me feel attractive, which probably had a lot to do with the massive hunk of grimy, rusty metal that sat beneath me. Oh, well. I never envisioned winning a girl over with my looks alone.

My dad drove Becca and me to the dance in our accessible van. We joked along the way about ways that we could convince our friends that we were actually dating. Upon dropping us off, my dad wished us a good time and told us he'd be in the same spot to pick us up when the dance ended.

The school gym was dark and filled with bodies. Smashed into the center of the floor was a huge pack of kids, bumping and grinding to the unexpectedly loud music. Farther from the center floated many smaller groups of friends—some dancing, others talking and laughing. The perimeter of the gym was reserved for loners, chaperones, and the two nerds playing an intense game of Pokemon underneath a set of bleachers. I took in this scene and lost most of the confidence I had worked up. This was clearly an event for able-bodied people, and I'm not sure why I imagined a DANCE would be any different.

Friends noticed our arrival and sprinted over to us, hugging Becca and smiling and waving at me. Jenny tried to make conversation with me.

"Hey, Shane! Are you ready to dance?" she asked excitedly, performing a few cute little moves in front of my chair.

"Definitely! I've been practicing my moves for a few weeks!" I yelled, battling the loud music.

"What?!" she yelled back, leaning closer and putting her ear to my face. I said it again, trying to be louder, but suddenly realizing that my puny voice was no match for the roar of the music. "I can't hear you! I'm gonna go dance!" she replied.

That sucked. It sucked more to look over at Becca and see that she and a few kids were in fits of laughter over a story one of them was telling. They were all perfectly capable of yelling loud enough to hear each other. My tiny body couldn't pull it off. From that point on, my interactions became pretty basic. Lots of one-word responses, exaggerated facial expressions (which became my one and only way of eliciting any type of reaction in a conversation), and head nodding. People tell me today that I communicate really well with my facial expressions. I mastered that skill over the course of a few years in middle school, as it became my only way to communicate with friends at all the loud events at which we often found ourselves at. That night, though, I felt particularly robbed of a great time. As my friends became aware of my volume difficulties, they (perhaps subconsciously) stopped trying to have conversations with me.

I danced with them, basically spinning my chair in circles and bobbing back and forth to the beat. We laughed and had a good time, but I couldn't shake the feeling that I was one step removed from everyone because of my inability to communicate. I pretty quickly gave up on trying to win the attention of any girls. What was I going to do? Nod at them for three hours?

Near the end of the dance, Becca came up to me and said, "Hey, can you let your dad know that I'm going home with Nicole? She's having a pool party sleepover. I already called my mom, and she said it was fine."

"Sure!" I yelled, nodding my head. Listening to everyone's conversation, I gathered that most of my friends were planning on sleeping over at Nicole's house that night. She was rich and had a beautiful inground pool. Someone eventually extended an invitation to me, but my immediate response was, "I can't tonight, I have plans. Sorry!" I didn't have plans, but I didn't want anyone to know.

The truth is that it was very difficult for me to sleep over at other people's houses at that age. Sleeping in my chair doesn't work, which meant I needed someone to lift me into a bed, as well as roll me from side to side throughout the night. Since I had never even met Nicole's parents, asking them to assume this responsibility wasn't something I was comfortable with. My other option was to go to Nicole's and ask my dad to pick me up late so I could just sleep at home. Never in my life have I been able to make this decision without feeling like an enormous burden on my parents, since both of them have to wake up early for work each day. For that reason, my typical response throughout those years of my life was to just pretend I had other things going on. In reality, I'd be in bed by 10:30 p.m. so my parents could get a good night of sleep.

When my dad picked me up from the dance, he beamed with pride and asked if I'd had a good time. I told him I had, which wasn't a lie. Despite some of the annoying aspects of my first middle school dance, I was still there, which felt like a big step toward achieving that much-desired sense of normalcy that my young mind so deeply craved.

chapter 17

fun on the short bus!

Normalcy, however, was at times elusive. Luckily, the funniest things in life are the abnormal. Throughout middle school, I was forced to ride the short bus, simply because they were the only buses that had wheelchair ramps. Everyone knows that the short bus is for kids with mental disabilities. Many people do not know that short buses are also for kids like me.

As you can imagine, I didn't particularly enjoy riding the short bus, especially when I was young and insecure about fitting in with my peers, but as I got older I realized the events I observed on the short bus were hilarious, and my annoying situation became much more bearable. Whether it makes me a bad person is up for debate, but throughout middle school and high school, I spent most of my rides to and from school laughing discreetly to myself in the back of the bus.

Over the years, there were a few kids and particular experiences that have stuck with me. Some are funny. Some are disgusting. They are all completely bizarre. (All the names have been changed, by the way.)

There was Adam, or as he called himself, Skunk. I kid you not, this kid was so proud of his unbelievable stench that he referred to himself as Skunk. The bus driver, Jim, who knew how to joke around with the kids in a way that wouldn't upset them, greeted Adam every morning by saying, "Hey, Adam! Have you taken a shower yet?" Adam responded by laughing like a hyena that had just taken a hit of helium, and then screaming, "SKUNKS DON'T TAKE SHOWERS! THEY JUST GROOM THEIR SKUNK TAILS!"

Then Adam would giggle his way to the back of the bus and sit down in the seat in front of me, but on the opposite side of the aisle. I had a full view of Adam since my chair was a lot higher than the tiny bus seats. Why is this important? Well, despite being a skunk, Adam was, in his heart, a bit of an exhibitionist. On almost every bus ride, Adam would have a conversation with himself that would inevitably lead to him pulling his penis out to share with the world. The first time this happened, I was just sitting there, minding my own business, and all of a sudden I noticed he had his penis completely out of his pants, just chilling on his lap. He was scanning the bus with a huge smile on his face, trying to catch someone's attention. Our eyes met and his smile got even wider, his plan was a success. I yelled at him immediately,

"DUDE! What the hell are you doing? JIM! Adam has his dick out! Dude, put that away!" Adam was as happy as could be, and his hyena laughter covered up the sound of the bus driver yelling at him. His dick remained out in the open until we got to school. I stared out the window and pondered why my life was so ridiculous.

Skunk made flashing a daily ritual, but eventually he grew bored with just grossing the hell out of me, so he began stepping up his game. He'd stand up while the bus was moving, and walk up to the other kids, attempting to smack them with his package! There was only one time when Adam approached me with his penis. I verbally kicked the shit out of him, so harshly that he stopped in his tracks, his jaw dropped like one in a cartoon, and he returned to his seat. When you can't physically defend yourself, you develop other methods. Adam never tried to mess with me again.

Obviously, the bus driver could not allow this craziness to continue, so he began threatening to tell the principal at our school about what Adam was doing, which is a conversation I would have loved to hear. This threat terrified Adam, and he always responded in the most peculiar fashion, yelling, "NO, NO, NO, NO! I'll just curl up in my turtle shell and eat some carrots!" He would then zip his coat up over his head, pull his arms inside, and presumably play with his shlong for the rest of the ride, because he always pulled *that* into his turtle shell as well.

Then there was Justin the superhero. Justin had superhuman

strength and was constantly getting into arguments with the tiny kid who sat next to him. These arguments always ended with Justin picking the other kid up and literally throwing him into the seat behind him. One time he tried to jump out of the closed bus door while the bus was moving. When Jim yelled at Justin for misbehaving, Justin apologized by howling at the top of his lungs, like a wolf howling at the moon. Fun facts: Justin always wore shirts that featured images of wolves howling at the sky, and he knew every word to every song in every Disney movie ever made.

Mike and Zack sat next to each other near the back of the bus. I'm not exactly sure what the name for Mike's condition is, but he used an assistive walker to get around, and all of his movements seemed to be in super-slow motion. It was obvious that his mental functions were affected by whatever he had, but not so much that I considered him "mentally disabled." He could hold intelligent and engaging conversations, but he spoke slowly and with a pretty bad speech impediment. Mike was honestly a cool dude, and I enjoyed talking to him when he occasionally sat in the back near me.

Most of the time, however, Mike sat with a kid named Zack, who, as far as I could tell, just had a mental condition that made him obnoxiously irritating all the freaking time. For example, there was a solid three-week period when Zack did nothing but rap the chorus of John Cena's introduction song from WWE as loud as he could the entire way to and from school. He didn't even stop when Jim gave him money to be quiet.

Anyway, cool and quiet Mike sat with loud and annoying Zack and the two of them got along really well most of the time, until they started wrestling.

One day I overheard Mike telling Zack that he was taking a special karate class with a private instructor. I can't even imagine how Mike did karate; it took him a few minutes to put his book bag on. Nevertheless, he claimed that he was getting really good at karate and that he wanted to show Zack some karate moves. The mini-karate lesson that ensued was painfully awkward; Zack was a hundred times better at karate chopping and arm-twisting because he was significantly faster and stronger than Mike. Initially, Zack allowed Mike to demonstrate the karate moves on him, but pretty soon Zack grew bored with the slow motion instructions, and started doing his own karate moves on Mike. At first, Zack was just messing around, pretending to punch, slap, and karate chop Mike very gently, but again Zack got bored. He started legitimately hitting Mike, who couldn't put up any kind of defense. Mike seemed like he was enjoying the fight though, despite the fact that he was basically a human punching bag. I decided they were getting out of hand when Zack punched Mike in the jaw hard enough to knock his glasses off.

"Whoa, Zack! Chill out man. You guys probably shouldn't do that." I said in a stern voice that I hoped would intimidate them into stopping. However, Mike replied, "No, it's okay . . . I'm fine. We're just playing."

Fine. You want to get your teeth knocked out, be my guest. I stopped paying attention. Unfortunately, I felt obligated to step in a few more times over the next few days because I couldn't be silent and watch Mike take the ridiculous beatings that Zack was giving him. Every time I tried to stop them, Mike told me he was fine and he was having fun. Jim eventually caught on to what they were doing after a few weeks, and he tried his best to keep them separated, but they still found ways to fight when he wasn't looking. Mike's desire to be hit is something I will never understand. Maybe he was deeply moved by the movie *Fight Club*.

Last, but certainly not least, was Brandon, a kid who lived in a neighborhood that was basically on top of a mountain. Therefore, the roads we had to take to get to his house were very steep.

The temperature inside the bus on this one very hot and humid May day felt like we were sitting in an oven while we waited for the rest of the kids to board at the end of the day. Brandon, who was rather large and somewhat clumsy, got on the bus and plopped himself down in the front row. Brandon was in his early twenties, but because of his mental disability, he behaved like a young child, which is why he was allowed to remain at our high school after his senior year. He also smelled like he always had a large pile of poop in his pants, which might have been because he always had a large pile of poop in his pants.

We pulled out from the school and headed for the house on the hill. On the way there, Brandon started complaining that he was too hot and felt dizzy, but Brandon was always being overly dramatic, so everyone pretty much ignored him. As we got closer to the house on the hill, Brandon doubled over in his seat and moaned that he wasn't feeling so well.

And then he immediately proceeded to throw up an astonishing amount of God-knows-what into the aisle of the bus. All the kids screamed and the bus driver cursed and said he had to get to the top of the very steep hill we were currently on before he could stop. I watched in horror as the puddle of vomit started sliding to the back of the bus toward me. The smell, amplified by the heat and humidity, was too much to handle. I held my breath as the puddle made its way back to me and settled right next to my wheelchair. There were chunks of fucking corn in the vomit. The bus driver didn't even clean it up when we got the top of the hill because the emergency supply kit was lacking a mop. In fact, I had to sit next to that steamy, chunky, putrid puddle of puke for the rest of the forty-five-minute bus ride. Riding the short bus was such a blast.

chapter 18

wheelchair adventures

Although at times I've hated the implications of being in a wheelchair, I've also found many ways to enjoy the hell out of it. Obviously, the way I play sports is a little different, actually a lot different, than the way most people play, but I have found a way to involve myself in almost every sport my friends have ever played.

In my toddler years, I went through the normal phase of wanting to go fast all the time. So while my childhood friends were riding their Big Wheels and tricycles as fast as they could down our back alley, I was racing right next to them in my wheelchair. My mom allowed me to ride around our neighborhood at a pretty young age, and from that point on, my friends and I spent hours on end being NASCAR drivers, as we raced as fast as we could around the block until the sun went down. My brother learned to ride a bike without training wheels when he was three years old, so he quickly joined us in our daily adventures.

It was during these days of nonstop play that I mastered driving my wheelchair at its top speed, which is twelve miles per hour. Cops and robbers is basically just another name for tag, so I developed the ability to chase people at top speeds, all while constantly monitoring their speed to assure I didn't slam into them and kill them if they stopped quickly or changed directions. Today, people are always amazed by how well I handle my wheelchair, and I have to give all the credit to my childhood days of chasing my friends around our block.

Naturally, as we got older we became more interested in sports, and our games of cops and robbers turned into games of football, basketball, soccer, baseball, and hockey. When we played football, I was usually on defense all the time. Since we didn't have any really big grassy areas to play on, our football games were two-hand touch anyway. We adapted the rule so that all I had to do to "tackle" the ball carrier was get my wheelchair within a foot of his legs. This got really dangerous when my friends were running around at full speed, and I was trying to get within a foot of them without running them over. When someone on the offense ran out to catch a pass, they had to deal with the 400-pound wheelchair flying toward them while they tried to catch the ball. Every once in a while I would accidentally nail someone in the shins, which was enough to cause them to fear me for the rest of the day. I didn't like to play offense when we played football because all I could do was run with the ball, and I knew my friends were faster than my wheelchair, so if I ever scored a touchdown, it would only be because they let me, and I hated that just as much as they did.

When my brother was in seventh and eighth grades, he played on our church's basketball team with a bunch of kids who had no idea how to run in a straight line without falling, let alone dribble a basketball or do anything close to productive on a basketball court. I had to do community service for my high school's graduation requirement, so I volunteered to help coach the team. It was hilarious watching these kids try to learn the offensive plays, when a majority of them barely knew how to make a layup. I will be honest; I spent most of the time laughing with my brother about how much of a joke the team was. My brother is a decent basketball player, however, he was not nearly good enough to carry the team in games against other churches, and I think we may have won four games total during my two-season tenure. The guy who was in charge of the entire league made a really big deal out of presenting me with a Coach of the Year award during halftime at one of the games. It was an extremely nice gesture by him, but I felt bad because he and most of the spectators in attendance didn't realize how much of a joke I made out of coaching this team. All they could see was a kid in a wheelchair who hung around with the team and was an amazing individual for wanting to coach despite his disability.

Baseball was difficult to play just for fun, so as kids we played a lot of Wiffle ball. I can't bat, throw, or catch, but baseball is my favorite sport, so whenever we played, I would pinch-run for my friends. Basically, I just made a huge deal out of the base-running aspect of baseball. I stole bases like Ichiro. Honestly, though, I got just as much enjoyment out of watching and being the umpire.

As we grew up, my brother realized he was actually really good at baseball and spent most of his summers playing on various teams. He and I spent a lot of time discussing and practicing baseball when he wasn't playing for a team.

When I was about ten or eleven, my parents found out about a baseball league designed for people with severe disabilities, whether they be physical or mental, and suggested I try it out.

The league was called Challenger Baseball League and their motto could have been something like, "Where everyone wins!" I showed up to the first game in my bright orange uniform, totally excited to kick some ass. I was in for a rude awakening. One of the first things I noticed while we were waiting for all the players to arrive, was that all the kids seemed more disabled than me. (I am not making fun of these kids, just telling you the truth.) Most of them were either talking to themselves, drooling, having severe tantrums, or trying to escape from their wheelchairs. I immediately felt out of place.

"Let's use the heaviest bat we can find for the picture of the kid without muscles."

Once both teams had gathered, the coaches started explaining the rules. The first was that each kid was accompanied by a parent at all times, whether batting or playing the field. That made sense; I had planned on my dad helping me do the physical stuff, and on the way to the game we had even discussed how I was going to quickly communicate to him where to throw the ball when we were in the field. I made him repeat to me that I would always want him to try to get the lead runner out, unless we had the chance to twist a double play.

The rest of the rules were: Nobody was ever out. Every batter got to bat once an inning, run the bases, and score. Also, there was no score being kept. Are you kidding me?

That last rule caught me way off guard. This was becoming no fun, and we hadn't even started playing. And when we did eventually begin, it got so much worse. I was the first player up to bat, and my dad helped me hit a slow ground ball to a kid in a wheelchair at shortstop. This particular kid had some kind of disorder that caused his head to be constantly moving in all directions, and it was very obvious he didn't really know what was going on as his mom moved him to the ball and picked it up to put in his lap. Meanwhile, I was booking it down the line to first. I stopped at first base, kind of disappointed that his mom hadn't tried to throw me out. Although it's probably good that she didn't, because the kid playing first was playing with the dirt. For a second, I stayed on first and thought, "Wow. This is stupid." And then it got even stupider. The fans, coaches, and parents helping out were still cheering for me. It took me a moment to realize what was going on, but then it clicked, they wanted me to keep running the bases. Nobody was even going to try to get me out. So I reluctantly began toward second base, not even bothering to go fast, proceeded on to third, right past the kid with the ball on his lap, and eventually made my way to home plate. It was the most degrading and unrewarding feeling I had ever felt up to that point in my life. Everyone worked together to *let* me get an inside-the-park home run on a ball that barely made it past the pitcher's mound. All the parents and coaches emphatically congratulated me like I was safe at home because of my chair-driving ability. I didn't have to say anything to my dad; he knew I was completely done with this league.

Unfortunately, he made me stick out the rest of the season to teach me the lesson of finishing what you start, but we spent most of the games making fun of how god-awfully fake and unrealistic the games were. Don't get me wrong, I think the Challenger League is a great program for lots of kids; it provides a unique experience for many disabled kids who all really enjoy it, but the fact that it felt so fake to me made it impossible to enjoy.

A couple years later, my parents managed to talk me into joining a "Challenger" style, bowling league. To bowl, I use a ball ramp that is available at most bowling alleys. Basically I just line it up by bumping it with my wheelchair and then push the ball down. Challenger bowling was fun for a couple weeks, until a kid in my lane had a severe seizure during laser bowling. That was the end of me trying to participate in sports leagues with my wheelchair brethren. I just couldn't fit in or have fun with those kids. I'm probably an asshole.

chapter 19

the pimple days

Whenever anyone asks about the buttons on my wheelchair, my automatic response is, "That button is for the rocket launchers." That way, if the person replies, "Wait, really?" I know we are never going to be friends.

I attended Freedom High School in Bethlehem, PA, which was located a mere three hundred yards from my middle school. For most of my life, the school had simply been a building, a landmark. My friends and I used to skateboard on the staircases that surrounded the premises. Well, I watched them skate. Pat and Andrew and I also spent many days smashing tennis balls at each other on the Freedom tennis courts.

Entering the building as one of its two-thousand-something

students for the first time my freshman year was an eye-opening experience. I was captivated by the immensity of it all and felt much older all of a sudden, if for no other reason than all the people around me looked much older.

I took it upon myself to make sure that my cousin Becca and I were together as much as possible in high school. Because of my disability, the law says the school has to put together a plan of all the adaptations I needed for each school year. Throughout all four years of high school, my disability plan had a clause that stated that I could request to have Becca in my classes if it was possible to coordinate our schedules. We justified it by saying that Becca was the only one who knew how to help me out, which was bullshit, but it allowed us to be together!

Another clause of my disability plan stated that I was allowed to leave class five minutes early before lunch, and five minutes early at the end of the day, in order to avoid the ridiculously packed hallways of our high school. I was also allowed to leave class to go to the nurse's office, which is where I went to use the bathroom. Jesus Christ, did we abuse those privileges.

During high school, I never once went to the nurse's office to use the bathroom, because that would mean the middle-aged school nurse would have to handle my shwang, which in my mind was far worse than holding it all day. Besides, I can hold my pee like it's my job. However, none of my teachers knew this, so when Becca and I got tired of sitting in class, I politely asked to be excused to the nurse's office, and Becca would escort me because I said I needed her to come with me, and nobody ever questioned that line of reasoning. Then we would walk around the school until we felt like we were pushing the limits of how long it should take me to pee.

Similarly, we often came up with ridiculous reasons for why I needed to leave earlier than five minutes before the end of the day, such as, Shane has to get his jacket on, or, the elevator is broken so we have to go outside and around the school to get downstairs, or, Shane has to pick up something from the nurse. We could pretty much do whatever the hell we wanted by involving the nurse's office in our excuse. Teachers automatically believed any reason I needed to go to the nurse, which I had marked up as a plus for being disabled.

Okay, so maybe I didn't really mature very much in high school, but I had a good time!

In ninth grade I ran for class president and had to give a speech to the six hundred kids in my class to persuade them to vote for me. Up to this point in my life, only my close group of friends knew that I was a completely normal person that happened to be in a wheelchair. Everyone else assumed that my wheelchair meant I was socially inept. Anyway, I wanted to start high school by making people aware that I was not either of those things. The following is an exact transcript of the speech I gave on election day. I almost got in trouble because I didn't read the speech I had handed in for the teachers to check. I don't know why I still have this saved.

> *sup im shane. i like to skate, i run track and field and i am on the freshman swimming team. at least . . . i was until the accident. anyway my buddy called me and told me a tsunami was about to hit and wipe out all humanity. so i decided to grab my surf board. holy hell was that a mistake. while on a seventy-five-foot wave i crashed into a cement wall. it is still unknown how and why there was a cement wall in the middle of the ocean, but that is not an important detail. when i awoke four years later from my coma, i was informed that i would never be able to walk again. i became a better man because of it. and in case you are stupid, the entire previous section is completely fictional. but for real i am in a wheelchair and if you decide to judge me for it, i will not hesitate to run you over until I'm sure you've stopped breathing. Vote for me!*

People went crazy, and I won the election by a landslide.

High school turned out to be much easier than I had anticipated. When I was in eleventh grade, I signed up for dual-enrollment classes at the local community college because I wanted to "get ahead" and be done with school as fast as possible. I had to take two placement tests, reading and writing, before they would let me sign up for Intro to Psychology. I was very nervous because these were *college* placement tests and I was only in eleventh grade, but they were ridiculously easy.

Here is a sample question from the test:

Which sentence uses a period correctly?

A. *I. Like. To. Eat. Pizza . . .*
B. *I like to eat pizza.*
C. *Pick B*
D. *Seriously, B is the correct answer, and you should pick it.*

I finished the tests and printed out the results; I got a 100 percent on the writing and a 98 percent on the reading because the painfully boring story about salmon migration patterns made me want to break the computer with my face.

Then, I had to take the test results to an old woman at her desk on the other side of the room so she could review my scores and tell me if I could sign up for the class I wanted. I drove over and awkwardly handed her the paper because I can't really hand people things; I just kind of push them off my lap. She took it and said, "Okay, honey, let's see how you did," as if I were a toddler that had just used the toilet for the first time.

Her face instantly changed to astonishment and she said, "Wow, I didn't expect this!"

"Uh, what?" was my reply. Was she joking? The salmon I had read about could have passed those tests. Then she realized how rude she had sounded and quickly added, "We just don't usually get scores like this! Congratulations!"

I know my body looks fucked up, but I honestly feel like there is no physical indication that would lead people to think I'm mentally disabled, and scenarios like the above are funny, but incredibly annoying. Instead of letting it bother me too much, I tried to have fun with the misperceptions many people had of me.

That same year there was a day when my friend Jon rode the short bus back to my house with me to chill after school. We were bored so he suggested we go on chatroulette.com. For those of you who have never heard of chatroulette (come out from under your rock), it is basically a web site where you can video chat with random people from all around the world. A majority of the people who use the site use it to satisfy their exhibitionist fantasies. In other words, you get paired up with lots of old, fat dudes jerking off. I wish I were joking. However, every once in a while you get the opportunity to have an actual conversation with someone from another state/country, which can be pretty interesting.

We went on chatroulette to see if we could find any good-looking girls to talk to, and to neither of our surprise, it was mostly dicks. Whenever we did come across fully clothed, normal people they usually said something along the lines of "What is wrong with that kid's head?" A douche bag British kid asked me to pull my sleeves down because my skinny arms were creeping him out. We decided I would scare away any girls that we might potentially have the chance of talking to, so Jon positioned the laptop so only he could be seen in the chat window. Our plan was to introduce me if someone seemed cool enough to not flip out.

Using this method, we came across a girl who looked to be about our age, and Jon started making small talk with her. I think she was from New York, but I could be wrong. She wasn't drop-dead gorgeous, but she wasn't ugly; her looks really had nothing to do with it at this point, we just wanted to talk to someone other than an old man. She told him she was bored too because she had to babysit her sister until her parents got home.

I whispered to Jon to introduce me and let me come into the video. Jon was a jokester, so he capitalized on this opportunity to do something funny. He told the girl that he happened to also be babysitting someone—his mentally disabled cousin. Initially, I think he just said it to fuck with me.

When he turned the camera to me, I put my T-Rex arms close to my chest, crossed my eyes, and tipped my big head to the side. She completely bought it; there was no reason not to. I can make myself look very deranged. She also expressed how bad she felt for me and how nice Jon was for babysitting me. I sat there pretending to drool.

To be completely honest, I don't know which one of us thought of our next move, so I will say we both thought of it/ agreed to do it. Jon said something along the lines of "Yeah, we are on here trying to find some boobs because this little guy has never seen them, but we're only finding old men on here." I made a sad face.

Try to understand how hard we were both resisting laughter at this point. The girl replied that I was so cute and that all the old men also repulsed her. In the heat of this comedic moment, Jon asked her if she felt like showing his mentally challenged cousin her boobs. I didn't know what to do so I just kept my mentally challenged face on and tried my absolute hardest not to laugh; I just wanted to see her reaction to his question, and then I would stop and reveal that I was messing with her and hopefully she would find it funny.

As if this whole situation was completely normal and happened to this girl all the time, she stood up, took the laptop into her bathroom, AND TOOK HER SHIRT OFF. Hello boobs.

Jon fell off the chair he was sitting on. I started incoherently apologizing repeatedly in between laughs of disbelief as I closed the Internet browser as fast as my T-Rex arms would let me.

I had just pretended to be mentally challenged to make a

girl show me her boobs. I don't know if it gets worse than that in terms of exploiting a disability.

We sat there stunned for a lengthy amount of time. Then we decided we were the worst people on earth and promised never to tell anyone ever.

chapter 20

an ode to darla

My insurance company covers a new wheelchair every six years. I'm guessing they didn't just pull that number out of thin air—although it wouldn't surprise me—but there probably was some research that found a wheelchair's life expectancy to be about six years. Imagine if that was your job: find out how much damage this wheelchair can take before it falls to pieces. I want that job.

Midway through high school, I became eligible for a new chair. For a few weeks, my parents, as well as my physical therapist, argued with me about getting a new one. Believe it or not, I really didn't like changing wheelchairs. I pretty much hated it. But when I told people this, it took them some time to understand where I was coming from. I said the word *new* but they heard the word *better*. However, new was not always better when it came to the seating arrangement that was such a crucial aspect of my everyday life.

One of the reasons that I was so against changing wheelchairs was that the able-bodied people who assist in the wheelchair selection and customization process have trouble understanding the intricacies of how I sit. For instance, a big point of contention was the fact that I lean so far to the right and put almost all my body weight on my right rib cage. It was a completely acceptable problem for the therapists and wheelchair representatives to be concerned about. However, and this is a big however, I physically can't hold my head up or move my arms if my body is adjusted even several inches to the left. When I explained this to them, they essentially ignored me and played the we're-specialists-so-we-know-better-than-you card. It was extremely frustrating, as they lifted me from one chair to the next, while I knew just by looking at each chair that it wasn't going to work.

They said things like, "Well, maybe if we reclined the chair, your body would naturally rest on the backrest rather than your side. Or maybe we should look into a head strap that will hold your head in place since you can't hold it up when you're in the proper position."

I responded, "But I would literally have to be almost fully reclined all the time, and I can't drive that way, so that wouldn't work. Also, I definitely do not want a head strap." Then came their line that filled me with so much anger that my eyes teared up, "Well, Shane, we might just have to compromise on this one."

It felt like they were ignoring everything I said. On top of that, to be told I was going to have to wear a head strap from then on, with no say in the decision, was more belittling than you can imagine. The fact is, the specialists were usually wrong. They've been telling me since I was four that I'm going to get skin breakdown from leaning on my right elbow all day, and that we should look into a bunch of different methods to take pressure off my elbow, methods that would render my right arm unusable. Every six years I fought them off and somehow convinced them that my elbow would be fine. Twenty-one years of leaning on my right elbow have gone by, and guess what, not once have I had any breakdown of the skin.

With a new wheelchair on the way (a process that would take four to five months because of stupid insurance hassles) I felt like the proper thing to do was take some time to honor the valiant life of my soon-to-be old wheelchair. We'd been through a lot together; some fun, some shit, but all worth remembering. So I wrote her this letter:

> Dear Darla,
>   The time has come to say goodbye. But before you go, let's reminisce about all the memories we've shared.

There were the countless feet that we have run over together. Most of the time it was an accident, but sometimes we did it on purpose and disguised it as an accident. Other times we ran over feet because people asked us to, not in a fetishy kind of way, more of a, "Run over my foot I want to see if it hur—OH GOD! GET OFF! GET OFF!"

There was the time we stayed outside in the summer downpour against all reasonable logic, and you broke down for three days. I had to sit in a very old, very uncomfortable, manual wheelchair while you were being repaired. Andrew parked me in the corner and told me I was in timeout probably a hundred times during those three days. Without instant Netflix, I probably would have died.

There was the time we were in the car together, not strapped in (because we like to live on the edge), and mom had to slam on the brakes and you rocketed toward the front of the van, since I had also forgotten to turn you off. I broke my big toe as we collided with the driver's seat, so that was a learning experience. We still don't strap you in, though, because we still like living on the edge, but at least I now remember to turn you off.

There was the time you threw me out of your seat when I ran over a soccer ball with you. The broken femur I suffered put me out of commission for a month. I still kind of hate you for that, but forgiveness is a process.

There were all the times we were an awesome street hockey goalie. Your four hundred pounds of steel and brute force, combined with my catlike reflexes and determination to win made quite an impressive team.

There was the time the street in front of our house froze over and we had races on the ice until my entire body was frozen solid.

There was the time I missed the birth of my firstborn son because I forgot to charge you the night before. (That never happened, but I have missed countless events because I'm an idiot and almost never remember to rejuice my battery at night.)

There was the time I burned holes in your controller interface because I wasn't paying attention while playing with fire with Andrew in the backyard. That's what I get for having such a fascination with fire.

We have traveled hundreds of miles together. We went through puberty together. We made friends together. I can never thank you enough for all that you've done for me. You will never be replaced. You will never be forgotten.

Unless, of course, my new chair is a lot cooler.

I don't actually name my wheelchairs. My wheelchair became Darla about fourteen seconds ago.

chapter 21

femur destruction

When I was in eleventh grade, I was forced to take an adaptive physical education class, much to my dismay (I just wanted to be in a normal class with my friends). This class consisted of two mentally challenged students and me. Not to imply that there's anything wrong with people who are mentally disabled, but honestly, both of these kids consistently smelled like they had atomic bowel movements simmering in their pants, and all they ever talked about was Disney movies. (Don't get me wrong, I love Disney, but I don't need to hear the storyline of *Finding Nemo* recounted to me over the course of an hour every single day of the week.) It was difficult for me to be enthusiastic in that situation, especially when my friends relentlessly joked that maybe I belonged in that class.

When I was younger, I could safely integrate myself into

whatever game our gym class was playing with only some minor adaptations. My friends always picked me to be on their teams. I never had to experience the trauma of being picked last. If we played a game that was particularly difficult for me, like Frisbee football or gymnastics, I would happily offer to sit out and be the "coach," which basically just meant sitting on the sidelines heckling and critiquing my friends' performances. But as we matured and entered high school, the level of play and competitiveness increased significantly. More often than not, I would choose to sit out and watch. If I did play, I knew that I would be a weight for my team to carry, ultimately hurting their chances of winning. Losing sucked, and I didn't want to be the one responsible for it. At the same time, it started to become dangerous for me to participate in fast-paced sports now that my friends were much taller and heavier than me. There were several occasions where I narrowly avoided death when students crashed into the side of my chair.

After a few days of the new adaptive PE class, I got over my distaste because I realized that I would be able to participate a lot more in this class, since I didn't have to worry about volleyballs or basketballs flying at my face at ninety miles an hour. There were no competitive games in this class. We went bowling and played beanbags and did modified versions of aerobics. Our gym teacher, Mr. K, was an awesome dude who shared my love for sports, so we often chatted about the Phillies while the other students played. My aversion to adaptive gym was further soothed when a few older cheerleaders volunteered to help out in the class. I stopped chatting with Mr. K and spent most of the class talking to them.

On a particularly warm day in October, our gym class decided to go outside. Usually this meant a painfully boring nature walk around the perimeter of the high school. I asked if we could bring a soccer ball out to mess around with, which is kind of ironic in hindsight, since Mr. K was the only one in the class who could actually kick the ball.

We went to the tennis courts and Mr. K took turns rolling the ball to each one of us. My method of passing the ball back to him involved driving my chair at the ball and bumping it with the front base of my wheelchair. I quickly became bored and asked him to give me some full-court passes that I would attempt to control and then pass all the way back. Piece of cake. All was going well and the cheerleader teacher assistants were impressed with my driving abilities. Then my gym teacher decided to kick me a different kind of ball. This ball was much softer than a normal soccer ball, so by the time it reached me on the other side of the court, it was carrying very little momentum, not enough for me to pass it all the way back to him. I stopped the ball with my wheel and then backed away from it until I was about twenty feet away. My plan was to gather some speed before I made contact with the ball.

In a moment that still seems unreal to me to this day, I drove my chair at top speed (ten miles an hour) toward the ball, but as I made contact, my front right wheel drove up over the ball due to its softness. My chair lurched to the side with a violence that I had never felt in all my years of driving. I lost sense of everything as my body was thrown out of my chair and came crashing down to the tennis court below. Blackness.

I opened my eyes and regained focus from a position that I did not often find myself in. Sprawled in a crumpled mess of atrophied body parts and blood, which was coming from my head, I began to make sense of where I was and what had just happened. I was lying on my side on the rough concrete of the tennis court, in a position pretty similar to how I lie in bed. I laughed uncontrollably as the absurdity of the situation set in, coupled with the delightful realization that I was alive. The laughter faded when I noticed Mr. K sprinting toward me in sheer panic. He was probably also relieved to discover me conscious and alive. I laughed again when he screamed for one of the cheerleaders to go to get help.

"Honestly, I really think I'm okay. What the hell happened? I guess I probably should have put my straps on. No, no, no. You don't need to get anyone. Nothing hurts that bad, except for my head a little bit," I told him, more concerned with avoiding the embarrassment of having more people see me in this vulnerable position than proceeding cautiously.

"Oh my God! Are you okay? Yeah, your head is bleeding. I don't really want to move you in case your back is injured. Oh my God. I think we should call an ambulance," Mr. K said.

"I'm seriously fine," I said, starting to get frustrated, "I have a metal rod in my back, so I don't really think it can break. Can you please just roll me onto my back? This concrete is killing my side." In the distance I saw one of the security guards running toward the tennis courts with the girl who had gone for help. Great, more hoopla.

Dramatic reenactment.

Then the fun began. After arguing with my gym teacher and the security guard for a few minutes, I was able to convince them to lift me back into my chair. Quite possibly the biggest mistake of my life. As Mr. K lifted my legs to maneuver me onto my back, a sharp pain shot through my right knee and radiated throughout the rest of my body. The first step to rolling me is sliding one hand under my knees. When he did this, it caused my legs to move approximately an inch, rising from the pavement to accommodate his hand sliding beneath them. This movement, the absolute slightest of fucking movements, hurt so badly that I shrieked. Literally shrieked. I can't even describe the sound I made in human words because the letters needed to create them have not been invented yet.

He frantically slid his hand out from under my knees, sending them plummeting from their inch of elevation to the pavement below. Another incomprehensible screech. I gathered myself and said, "I'm fine. I think I might have pulled a muscle in my right knee. Can you just pick me up from my side and put me back in my chair?" I'm an idiot. But apparently I'm a convincing idiot because Mr. K and the security guard only argued with me for several more minutes before agreeing to lift me back into my chair.

Spoiler alert: it was much more than a pulled muscle. My right femur was snapped in half just above my knee. I discovered that broken femurs don't support weight very well when the two adults hoisted me off the pavement using my knees and shoulders as lifting points. I'm not sure if you've ever felt the two sides of a broken bone separate from each other, but I would highly recommend it to anyone who would like to guarantee that they will never experience a sicker pain for the rest of their life. For dessert, I had the pleasure of feeling my bones rearrange themselves once again as my body assumed the sitting position of my wheelchair. Refusing to accept there was anything seriously wrong, I once again reassured the adults that I had only sustained a pulled muscle as we made our way to the nurse's office to get my bleeding forehead examined.

After inspecting the gash on my head and listening in horror to my recounting of the crash, the school nurse got my mom on the phone and strongly suggested we go to the hospital to have me checked. Concussions are apparently a bigger deal than I imagined. Even though the cut on my head did not require stitches, every adult involved in the situation agreed that I needed to be looked at by a doctor just to make sure my brain was intact. I kept the pulsing numbness in my right leg to myself while I waited for my mom to arrive with the van.

On the way out of the parking lot, Mom drove over a speed bump at an incredibly slow speed, which is how she normally navigates speed bumps due to my neck weakness—and the subsequent jostling doubled me over as my bones ground against each other inside my leg. Doubling over in agony resulted in an even more intense pain as the weight of my upper body pressed down on my fractured leg. I screamed like a madman. Mom probably thought the concussion test was looking like a great idea. The rest of the drive was a nightmare. I managed to communicate that my right leg was injured and that even the slightest bumps were causing me significant pain, but it just wasn't practical for her to drive five miles an hour the entire ten miles to the hospital.

The nurses had to cut my jeans off with a pair of scissors in the exam room at the hospital. In between desperate screams to be gentle and stabilize my leg, I warned the nurses—both very attractive—not to be alarmed if my dick was hanging out the bottom of my boxers. It happens. They laughed and then I returned to terrified scream sobbing. Did I mention that I was lying on a hospital bed at this point? No? That's probably because I'm repressing the memory of being lifted once AGAIN by my shoulders and snapped-in-half-femur leg.

In the X-ray room I finally lost my shit and strangled the technician who picked up my leg to reposition it for a better picture. May she rest in peace. She did not die in vain though; the ER doctor came in a few hours later to happily announce that, thanks to some very nice X-ray images, he was able to easily see that my femur had broken in a "corkscrew" manner just above my right knee. Big surprise. My parents and the ER nurses let out a collective squirm as they suddenly realized why lifting me by my legs had hurt so badly. Unfortunately, vindication doesn't heal broken bones. Neither does morphine, but it helps. A few minutes after being diagnosed, I floated off into a beautiful, morphine-induced dreamland.

I spent the next five days in the hospital. When my femur broke, the upper half of the bone shifted itself up and over the smaller segment that remained attached to my knee. Basically, the two pieces of bone collapsed over each other, shortening my upper leg significantly. After a series of arguments, many of which I was too zonked on morphine to comprehend, my doctors decided that my tiny, brittle, SMA bones could not support the stress of screws to correct the fracture. Instead, they reasoned, they would put me under anesthesia, set the bone as best they could, cast it, and hope for the best. Great. Whatever. Do that. Just give me more morphine.

Their plan failed. I woke up to a doctor apologizing to my parents, which, when you think about it, is never something you really want to wake up to. Apparently my bones didn't cooperate and they were unable to set them, so they decided to cast my leg as it was, a clusterfuck of mangled bones that was three inches shorter than my left leg. Upon hearing this I became aware of a massive bulge under my blankets. They had to cast me from hip to ankle, he explained, since the position of the break and my weak bones made my leg extremely fragile. A full leg cast was needed to keep the bones still during the healing process. He told me I would need to stay off of it, sitting included, for about a month. Fuck me sideways with a toaster. By this point I had been bedridden for two days—sleeping most of that time—and was already driving myself crazy with boredom due to my incapacitation. I wouldn't survive a month in bed.

I did.

A disabled kid who is stuck in bed all day is about as boring as it sounds. I watched a lot of television. My friends and family kept my spirits high with lots of visits, many of which were rather awkward considering the enormous cast and delicate leg made it impossible for me to wear pants or underwear. Really though, the moment that stands out to me the most from my time in recuperation, was pooping in a bedpan for the first time.

My parents gently rolled me onto my side, lifted my hips a few inches, and slid the bedpan (which was basically just a plate) underneath the unloading zone. I pushed. As my bowel movement came out, it pretty quickly reached the plate beneath me, but there was still a lot more left inside of me, which presented a dilemma. Should I chop it off and start a new log or keep going with the one I had? I opted to forge onward. As more came out, I felt the log coiling itself up on the plate. It had been a while since the last time I'd gone to the bathroom. This magnificent spectacle was taking place behind me, so I couldn't really see it, but I imagined that I was creating a perfectly little coiled up snake of a poop. It made all the pain I had endured entirely worth it, as did my dad's reaction when he came back in the room to find the cobra I had left for him.

chapter 22

drowning

It must have happened gradually, but at some point in high school, my right lung started to give up. I discovered this at a routine checkup in eleventh grade when the pulmonologist gave me a concerned look after listening with his stethoscope. "I hear some crackling, but nothing out of the ordinary for a partially collapsed middle lobe," he said with a nonchalance that confused me. What did that mean? Lungs should not be collapsed. They should be open and full of air and happiness. "Just means you might have some more phlegm buildup, so you'll have to be really careful about staying healthy," he said.

Winter was approaching, and my body was seriously worn down from the recent adventure with femur breaking. I worried I would get sick and be unable to fight it off. A collapsed lung? I could barely clear phlegm with fully functioning lungs, and now I might have to do so with only one good lung?

If worrying was an antidote, I might have gotten off unscathed that winter, but unfortunately, as I well knew, worrying didn't do much besides stress me out. A few days before Thanksgiving, I woke up with a tiny scratch in the back of my throat. My family and I went into Sickness Prevention Overdrive—bathing in gallons of Tylenol, sucking down copious amounts of breathing treatment mist, and performing constant chest percussion therapy (basically someone just smacks my chest for twenty minutes to loosen up the phlegm in my lungs. It's lovely).

Accidently put cocaine in my breathing machine.

The last-minute precautions failed, and the sore throat blossomed into a full-fledged case of bronchitis, a terrible illness for someone with my limited lung capacity. I wheezed my way through Thanksgiving dinner, barely able to hold my head up as my body was exhausted from the nonstop coughing. My airway felt like a pinhole, clogged with so much phlegm that breathing became the only activity I could handle.

My parents kept asking if I needed to go to the hospital, but I viewed the hospital as a place where people went to die. Accepting that I was too sick to get better by myself was accepting that I might die, and you'd be surprised by how difficult that made the decision.

Cough-drenched, sleepless nights and energy-draining days continued into December. The day after Christmas, I woke up very early in the morning and literally couldn't breathe. I sucked in as hard as I could, but instead of oxygen, all I got was a big mass of liquid phlegm gurgling in my trachea. Immediately I panicked and miraculously got my parents' attention with gargled cries for help. I probably sounded like I was drowning when they heard me. There was just too much phlegm in my airway. I needed air or I was going to pass out, so I signaled for Mom to roll me onto my other side.

I had been in this situation in the past. There were rare occasions before this when phlegm made it impossible to breathe, and rolling to my other side always shifted the mucus enough to open my airway just a tiny bit, allowing me to get that amazing inhalation of fresh air needed to clear the rest of it. It's kind of my go-to move when I am overwhelmed by phlegm.

Not this time. When I realized the roll had failed to move the phlegm, I lost my mind and began to cry. I was going to die. I didn't know what to do and everything was happening too fast and I really wanted to breathe and I really wished I had a normal life. All of those emotions hit me at once, with my bubbling gasps for air filling up the rest of the room. If you want to have a better understanding of how that felt and sounded, jump into a pool, sink to the bottom, and then try to breathe. (No, don't do that.)

In my state of complete panic and total desperation for air, I got Mom to sit me in my chair, thinking this might jostle the phlegm into a manageable position. My parents are masters of remaining calm in situations like this. Using all the strength I could muster, I coughed as hard as I could. Still no air.

As fast as my sickly Pterodactyl arms could move, I drove my chair to the living room and got Dad to hook me to the Cough-Assist machine. At this point it was pretty much like I was just holding my breath.

Wait . . . you have a machine that helps you cough? Why didn't you just use it right away?

It doesn't usually help me. The Cough-Assist is designed to push a large amount of air into my lungs all at once, and then suck all that air back out real fast. Therefore, when my airway is completely blocked with phlegm, all the machine does is push air against that chunk of phlegm, and nothing really happens. I tried coughing to the rhythm of the machine, while Mom smashed the mask into my face to create an airtight seal. It wasn't working, and in the whirlwind of thoughts that were rushing through my head, I heard my dad on the phone, making arrangements with the hospital to have me admitted.

Just when I was on the edge of giving up, and I hate to think about what would have happened if I had, the phlegm moved.

I whipped my head back, away from the mask, and inhaled the greatest breath of air I've ever taken. The phlegm was nowhere near gone, but there was an opening for just enough to get through and replenish my lungs. I collapsed back, allowed Mom to wipe my eyes, and simply relished the influx of fresh air. Nothing else mattered; it was just me, my lungs, and the beautiful, beautiful air.

chapter 23

marbles in my mouth

During my senior year of high school, I was in an honors English class, mostly because I was too lazy to take AP classes, but also because I enjoyed writing—even shitty school essays. We were told on the first day of class that since we were seniors and it was an honors class, we had to write a fifteen-page essay, as well as do a ten-minute presentation on a topic that we would derive from a fiction novel. When our teacher announced this assignment, my heart sank because of a new complication I had been having with my disease.

Rewind four years. I am in eighth grade, sitting in the school cafeteria, eating a burrito with my friends. At this point in my life, I had not given any consideration to the idea that my disease would slowly get worse as I got older. My disease is really good at fucking with my brain because it progresses so slowly that it is almost impossible to notice myself getting weaker.

In eighth grade, I knew that ten years ago I used to be able to sit in my sandbox and play without anyone holding me up; I knew that I used to be able to roll from one side to another while laying in bed when I was young, but I honestly didn't *feel* any weaker in eighth grade than I did in say, fifth or sixth grade. In my naïve, eighth grade mind, I reasoned that if I didn't feel weaker from one week to the next, I must be staying the same.

Then, about halfway through my burrito that day, my disease abruptly showed up to slap me in the face. One minute I was chewing my burrito, happy as can be, the next I was silently sitting there in utter confusion and terror, as my jaw muscles refused to continue chewing. At first, I thought my jaw had unhinged or something crazy like that, because as hard as I tried I could not get my mouth to move. I motioned for my friend to hand me a napkin to spit out the half-chewed burrito, playing it off to my friends as if something nasty was in that bite. "What the fuck just happened to me?" was all that went through my head the rest of that school day.

That night at dinner the same thing happened while chewing my cheeseburger, but in order to not freak out in front of my parents, I acted like I was resting my chin on my hands in an awkward way. I noticed that if I pushed up on my chin with my hands, chewing became much easier. All of a sudden it occurred to me; my jaw wasn't unhinged, but the muscles in my jaw were getting weaker. I was getting worse. Once in a blue moon I lie in bed and think "why me?" as I try to fall asleep. As pathetic as it sounds I usually end up tearing up and hating everything. This was definitely one of those nights.

By twelfth grade, I was using my hands to help myself chew at every meal. It became my normal way of eating, and I didn't think about it much. My friends occasionally imitated me because I look 100 percent ridiculous when I do it.

However, since that day in eighth grade, I had learned that my weakening jaw muscles also affected my ability to talk. I had developed a very slight mumble; my jaw and tongue get too tired to form words perfectly. Most of the time it is totally unnoticeable; once in a while people will ask me to repeat a word or something I say. Annoyingly, it has gotten to the point where I can't talk nonstop for an extended period of time. I am perfectly able to hold a conversation, where my mouth gets chances to rest while the other person is talking, but when I have to talk without pausing for any amount of time over about five minutes, my words become extremely garbled and are almost impossible to understand. Now you are beginning to see why I was upset about the ten-minute speech requirement; I was physically unable to talk that long.

I handled this situation in probably the worst way possible, by not telling anyone about my dilemma and trying to convince myself that I could do it. As the semester progressed, I worked superhard on my project. My paper was on satire and so I read *The Hitchhiker's Guide to the Galaxy*. My paper turned out really well and the slideshow I prepared for the presentation was actually funny and interesting.

Before my jaw muscles started getting really weak, I never got nervous talking in front of people, but this presentation went a long way in changing that.

In one of the final classes of the semester, I sat in extreme nervousness while a few other students presented before me. "Why didn't you just tell the teacher you couldn't do the speech?" was all I could think. My hands were sweating buckets as I realized I didn't know what I would do if my mouth started to fail me.

Finally it was my turn, so Becca and I made our way to the front of the class. I had asked her to help me click through my slideshow. The first three minutes of the presentation went pretty well, then, just as I had known the entire semester, my jaw started to freeze up. It got really bad really fast, and I could tell from my classmates' faces that nobody could understand me anymore. Then I made the situation even worse. I stopped speaking, turned to the teacher and mumbled, "My, uhhhh, mouth muscles are really tired . . . Umm, can I finish the rest of this tomorrow?" Sensing the awkwardness filling the room, my teacher replied, "Umm, yeah . . . okay, class, we're going to move on, and Shane will finish his presentation tomorrow." Every single kid in the class had the "oh God, this is awkward, look away" expression on their faces.

I went back to my seat, face reddening, and quickly

apologized to Becca for putting her through that. She couldn't stop laughing, and suddenly, neither could I. Sure, I was embarrassed to the point where my face felt like it was melting, but at the same time, I didn't care! Everything that had just unfolded was so completely awkward that it was hilarious. It would have been very easy for me to let that day break me down, but what good would have come from that?

I ended up getting an A on that presentation. That is what I call a pity grade.

chapter 24

getting drunk

Considering the fact that I weigh as much as the average seven-year-old, getting drunk never really seemed like a realistic possibility for me throughout high school. Actually, getting drunk wasn't the problem—it would probably only take a few sips to get completely wasted—but I was nervous about how my body would react to alcohol. Add to that the fact that my parents were the ones to put me in bed every night, and the situation becomes not just dangerous, but also extremely likely to land me in a pile of trouble. During winter break of my senior year, I finally convinced myself to take a risk and try it.

It was New Year's Eve. Becca and I were trying to spend as much time together as possible since we knew we wouldn't see each other very often once she went off to college at the University of Pittsburgh. We decided that we were going to spend New Year's Eve together, and attempt to get me wasted for the first time in my life. Normally, Becca would go out and party with her other friends on New Year's, and I would spend the night shoveling ungodly amounts of pork-fried rice into my tiny stomach with my family.

My disease makes drinking, or participating in any frowned-upon activity, a complicated matter. If I were going to stay out and drink, I would eventually have to call one of them to come get me, not to mention one of them would have to help me go to the bathroom and get into bed. Basically, it would be impossible to hide my drunkenness from them. Some of you might be thinking, so what, my parents know I drink and they don't care. My parents are not your parents, and they had a justified reason to not want me drinking; it was really unsafe.

I, however, had reached a point in my life on that New Year's Eve where I did not really care how dangerous drinking might be for someone of my condition. It seemed silly for me to go through life constantly making cautious decisions to avoid getting in trouble or hurting my body. You only have one life to live, might as well make the most of it.

But please don't get the impression that I was approaching this night by throwing all caution to the wind. I firmly believed that if I acted smart and responsible about drinking, everything would be absolutely fine. There was a small voice in the back of my head saying, "Remember, you are far from indestructible, and it would be just plain stupid to throw away a great life for one night of fun." I had no idea how much alcohol my liver could handle, and I wasn't about to test its limits.

We decided it would probably be easiest to enact Operation Get Shane Drunk at Becca's house, and that I would just sleep there to avoid confronting my parents while I was slizzard. The only bad part about this plan was that sleeping over at other people's houses was not very comfortable for me. Unless my brother was with me, I usually slept in my chair so that I didn't need to call anyone during the night to roll me from side to side. My chair is comfortable to sit in, as for sleeping . . . not so much. It did have a recline feature, but sleeping in it is far from desired. Also, I couldn't really go to the bathroom at other people's houses, again unless my brother is there who knows how to do all that fun stuff. I just wasn't comfortable with people outside my immediate family helping me with my overnight routine. If only I had considered all this before we decided to spend the night at her house.

Becca and I stopped by our grandfather's house before we went to her house, because some of our extended family was in the area and they were having a New Year's party. Around 10 p.m., we said goodbye and told everyone that Becca was having a couple people over to her house, which wasn't a complete lie; one of our other friends did join us for the festivities. As we left the party, my dad and our uncles came outside with us and reminded us to be smart about whatever we chose to do that night. I was surprised by the apparent fact that my dad was cool with me getting drunk as long as I wasn't stupid.

An adult who shall remain anonymous bought us a box of Franzia, which might be the classiest adult beverage of all time. We weren't trying to impress anyone.

When we got to Becca's house, the movie *300* was on TV, so we played a game where every time we felt intimidated by a character in the movie, we took a drink. Becca had to help me tip the cup to my mouth because the awkwardly shaped wineglass did not work well in my awkwardly shaped hands. After I finished my first full glass, I didn't feel any effects of the alcohol, and we started discussing the possibility that my SMA made me some kind of superhuman alcohol tank. Then I had another glass.

All of a sudden I was drunk. It was awesome. I felt so light and my muscles didn't feel as tight as they usually do. Our friend Brian showed up. He and Becca continued downing glasses of the delicious Franzia, while I practiced driving in straight lines around the room, which was impossible. We laughed a lot, mostly at me, and all in all it was a great time.

I've been told I can be arrested for DUI if I drive my wheelchair while drunk. Something about this seems unfair.

However, we didn't quite plan the whole night out as much as we should have. Around 3 a.m., Becca and Brian were absolutely smashed. They both wandered off to different parts of the house and passed out. I realized I was now alone downstairs, not drunk enough to pass out, and with only my phone to keep me occupied. I tried to sleep, but like I said, my chair is not very comfortable. Also, when I do sleep in my chair, I am usually very close to other people I can wake up if my head gets stuck or I become way too uncomfortable. Becca was two staircases above me and our other friend was nowhere to be found. (I later found out he had passed out in the guest bedroom, which was right next to the room I was in, so I could have gotten him if I needed to.) Anyway, at the time, I felt totally alone and didn't want to fall asleep for fear I'd wake up in pain and be unable to get someone's help.

I literally sat there and played games on my phone until it died. That was around 4:30 a.m. After that, I just sat there and tried to relax until somebody woke up. Not fun.

To my surprise and delight, Becca and her mom (oh God, I didn't even remember her mom coming home last night) both got up around 7 a.m. Becca came downstairs to get a drink because she was feeling really sick. I explained that I had yet to fall asleep and even though I acted like it was all good, her mom heard me talking and suggested they run me home so I could sleep. I say "they" because Becca had to drive my accessible van, and her mom had to follow us to bring

Becca back home. Needless to say we were all grumpy, and in retrospect Becca probably wasn't in the best condition to be driving. On the way home Becca and I started joking about the previous night. Becca found a video on her phone that we had forgotten about; it was just of me, sitting in my chair, with my head bobbing in all directions and a huge smile on my face. We laughed really hard.

I got home and woke up my dad, who was surprised by how early I was home. He didn't ask questions, but I told him about my night and he laughed a little. I wasn't sure if he'd be mad about me drinking, but he didn't seem to be. (When my mom found out later that day, though, she was not pleased.) I went to bed. My memory foam never felt so good.

Overall, that New Year's Eve was fun, but could have been a lot better if we had planned ahead.

chapter 25

college

I goofed off more than I should have in high school. None of the work we were given, even in honors classes, was particularly difficult. Most assignments were tedious and extensive at worst, but we all found shortcuts and loopholes and ways to split up the work to make our lives easier. Becca and I probably should have received a single high school diploma when we graduated, because there weren't many assignments that we did separately. Since we sat next to each other in most of our classes, and spent most of our time outside of school together, we cheated. A lot. We both felt that if we understood the material we were working on, there was no harm in splitting an assignment fifty-fifty to maximize productivity. Some of our teachers even knew about it, and would joke that we should receive the same grade on all of our assignments. Sometimes our cheating methods got a little ridiculous, as in, Becca would do all the math home-work and I would do all the science and then we would swap. Cheating on tests was a little more difficult. Luckily, we were able to sit relatively close to each other during exams, since she had to help me flip the pages of the test (which I could do completely on my own).

I got mostly As with little effort, and an occasional B when I didn't even feel like putting in that minimal effort. Then I woke up one morning of my senior year and realized I had no idea what I wanted to do with my life, or where I was going to go to college, or if college would even work for me, or what I wanted study. The real world scared me, and I didn't feel prepared in the least bit.

After some extensive conversations with my parents, we decided a local college would be my best option, so I could live at home and commute. I've never been taken care of for more than a few days by anyone other than my parents, and moving away would mean arranging full-time caretakers, which is expensive, stressful, and annoying. It felt a little un-fair knowing that many of my friends would be leaving their parents and going off to explore a new place in the world on their own, while I'd pretty much be doing things the way I had been my whole life, but with new friends and new classes. I wanted to be free. Had I been dead set on making that leap and leaving home, we probably could have figured it out, but fear of the unknown was also a pretty big factor for me. I was afraid of getting stuck with some old grumpy nurse named Gretchen who would make me go to bed at 9 p.m. and who wouldn't know the right way to wipe my butt after I pooped.

My college selection process was short lived and bittersweet. As it turned out, I visited, applied to, and chose to attend a grand total of one school—Moravian College in Bethlehem, PA, about four minutes from my house. Our family had a deep history at Moravian. My father went there, as did pretty much all my aunts and uncles. My grandfather, who I greatly respect for his ridiculous intelligence, taught English at Moravian for forty years. I knew the college would be welcoming when the first admissions counselor I talked to went into a long story about how my grandfather had been his favorite professor.

Being a private college, the tuition was pretty steep, but one of the scholarships they offered was for students related to alumni. That scholarship, combined with a few other awards for my grades and being disabled (I knew it would pay off someday) made the school a financial reality. If you want to go to Moravian, my parents told me, we can make it work.

The college was small, with only about three hundred kids per graduating class. It certainly wouldn't fulfill the desire I had to move on to a brand-new world of excitement and immensity like my friends would be getting at Duke and Penn State and Clemson. But at the same time, there was something enticing about the familiarity of knowing most of my classmates, of eating lunch in a quaint little cafeteria with a fireplace, of only having to travel a few hundred feet to get to each building. On top of that, Moravian is a liberal arts college, and although I was clueless about my future, I knew I wanted to write. Moravian would make me a well-rounded individual, not only helping me harness my writing abilities, but also teaching me to think critically and creatively.

The cheese fries in the cafeteria also caused me to have an involuntary orgasm the first time I had them, so really, I didn't have much of a choice.

I applied, sent them my SAT scores (which were somewhat above average, but not so above that I want to brag), and was accepted! It wasn't my dream school, and I still wish I could have gone away to somewhere awesome like the University of North Carolina, but it was a great fit for me and, more important than anything else, it was realistic.

I then went back to goofing off, perhaps even harder than before, for the rest of my senior year. As summer came and started to fade, more and more my friends spent their time being excited about college, getting ready, shopping for their dorms, and packing up. I was experiencing very different feelings as my summer drew to a close. More than anything, I was nervous. What if I didn't meet anyone cool at Moravian? What if nobody wanted to be my friend? What if I was the weird kid?

So as everyone started to head off in August, I got online and looked through the Moravian Class of 2014 Facebook page that someone had created. I posted a little introduction to myself, like other people were doing, and mentioned my disease and that I was looking for some people to eat lunch with, since I would need some help. A week later I had heard back from only one person. Fuck. I didn't really want to go to college anymore. Everyone would surely want nothing to do with me. I used to get discouraged pretty easily.

At orientation weekend, I started to really regret my decision to attend Moravian. The incoming freshmen were divided into small groups for a few days of tours and lectures and icebreaker type activities. Not my cup of tea to start with, but even lamer because it seemed like all the interesting, sociable people had attended a secret meeting and decided to talk only to one another during orientation. After a few painfully awkward conversations with painfully awkward individuals, I chose to skip some of the planned activities for the weekend, telling my parents they were optional.

At the final event of the weekend, a presentation by some author I had never heard of, things finally turned around. The lecture was held in an auditorium, where the only wheelchair accessible seating was down on the floor in the very front, separated from the rest of my class. Great. I sat alone for a few minutes and entertained myself by imagining the reaction I could get if I drove my chair onstage when the author started his talk.

Then suddenly there was someone next to me.

"Hey, man, what's up? I'm Jesse. I saw your post on Facebook, and I saw you like some awesome music. So I just wanted to come say hi."

Jesse sat down near me and we started talking about music. His jeans were skin tight, so he was obviously cool. By the end of our conversation, we were whispering because the author had started his talk. Jesse gave me his number, and we planned to eat lunch the first day of classes. The relief I felt in that moment was incredible. Maybe college wouldn't suck a thousand dicks after all. Over the next few weeks, Jesse introduced me to the friends he had made, and they welcomed me into their group. Those kids would become my closest friends over the next few years.

chapter 26

head fall

Since my body lacks the protein that is vital to the creation and sustainment of muscles, working out serves no purpose because I can't build new muscle tissue, but at the same time, never using my muscles causes them to disintegrate faster. It is kind of terrifying to imagine the muscles in my body slowly wasting away and knowing there is nothing I can do about it.

For most of my life, my neck has been my strongest body part. Whenever I am awake and sitting in my chair, I am using my neck muscles to keep my head balanced and upright. My wheelchair has a headrest, but the way I sit in my chair creates a half-foot gap between my head and the headrest. If I try to lean back to rest my head against the headrest, I lose my balance and my head falls backward into a position that looks and feels completely embarrassing. When my head falls into this awkward position, I don't have the strength to pick it back up, and I have to ask someone to push my head back up into position.

Until a few years ago, I never had to worry about my head falling over except when my friends drove my van and forgot that their severely disabled friend was riding in the back. However, more recently I have noticed my neck muscles getting slightly weaker, and my head has been falling over more often. It is difficult to explain the loss of dignity that accompanies losing the ability to lift up your own head. I have tried to accept the fact that this is my life and crap like this is inevitable, but when holding my head up was one of the few things I could do all by myself and it started to slip away, I became very frustrated.

When my head falls over in public, I laugh and act like it doesn't bother me, but in reality my mind is screaming, "Fuck! Fuck! Fuck! Fucking fuck!" A delusional part of my brain tries to convince me that people view me as a somewhat normal individual until they witness my head topple over, then they realize how truly different I am.

On my first day of college, I rolled into my first class, knowing almost nobody and nervous as shit that I would remain friendless through the next four years. I pulled my chair up next to a kid and asked if I could sit by him. He agreed and we briefly chatted until the professor walked in and began class. So far, in my mind I had assessed the situation as a success; the kid sitting next to me wasn't being awkward about my disability and now that class had started I patiently waited for a chance to answer a question in a way that would show the other students I was not mentally challenged. I know, I have some odd insecurities.

Anyway, as the class proceeded, the professor started writing some notes on the chalkboard. Suddenly, his piece of chalk broke and fell against the metal chalk holder below. I must have been daydreaming because the sudden loud noise was enough to make my body flinch. I was unprepared for the flinch and sure enough, I lost balance of my head and it started to fall. Using all the strength I had, I tried to keep it upright, but I didn't react fast enough and my head fell all the way back. If you want a mental picture of what I looked like, tip your head back as far as you can and keep it there. I was now sitting in class with my head stuck in that position.

It felt like every single person in the classroom was staring at me, probably because most of them were. Only about thirty students were in this particular class, so the small classroom made it all the more obvious. There was no way my professor didn't notice, but he continued the lecture as if nothing had happened. For a moment, I sat there with my head back, as the situation sank in. It might not seem like a big deal, but in that moment I reasoned that I would probably never make friends during college; people would never feel comfortable approaching me. Then reality hit and I needed to decide how I was going to get my head upright, because having my head so far back is also kind of painful. The kid next to me was either completely oblivious to what had just happened, or pretending he didn't notice. The following is the whispering conversation we had as I awkwardly tried to get help without drawing more attention to myself:

Me: Dude...can you like...push my head up for me...I'm stuck [awkward fake laugh].
Kid: Um, what?
Me: [quiet but real laugh as I realized how ridiculous I must look] My head fell. Can you push it forward?
Kid: Umm, I don't know...how?
Me: Just put your hand behind my head and bring it forward.

He did what I asked, but didn't push my head far enough forward for me to regain balance, and it fell right back to where it was before. It took him two more tries until my head was in the right position. I thanked him and sat there feeling utter embarrassment and guilt for putting him in that situation. Luckily, my head fell only a few times throughout the rest of college, and each of those times, I was next to a friend who laughed at me but also knew how to help me up.

chapter 27

an evening with michelle

During my sophomore year, my good friend Lily surprised me with an awesome phone call. "Shane, Michelle Obama is speaking at Moravian! I got you a ticket. You're coming with me."

I'm usually pretty hesitant to commit to going to events before doing my own research. (Is the venue accessible? Will there be a handicap seating area? Will I be able to see from that area? Will my nondisabled friends be able to sit with me in the handicap section?) However, Lily quickly convinced me that an event of such prominence would obviously be accessible, and that this was a once-in-a-lifetime opportunity, and that we wouldn't be friends anymore if I didn't attend. Needless to say, I said yes.

In the van on the way to the speech, Lily and I speculated about what the seating arrangements would be like. I've been

Dannen
P

Pickup By:
3/10/2020

Dannen b

Pickup By:
3/10/2020

.

.

.

.

.

.

to plenty of sporting events, concerts, speeches, and shows in my life to know that the handicap seating area is an often-overlooked section of many venues. Michelle was going to speak in the basketball gym at Moravian, a smaller-ish building that does not have a built-in handicap area. I would be sitting somewhere on the floor, probably near the front, I hoped, so I could see the stage. My biggest concern anytime I go to a public event is that the handicap section will allow me to sit with at least one of my able-bodied friends. Let's be honest, if you went to a football game with a bunch of friends, and found out upon arrival that you had to sit in a secluded area with a bunch of strangers while the rest of your friends sat together somewhere else, you would be at least slightly pissed. This has happened to me more than once, and it is indeed a pile of horseshit.

I must have expressed this mentality, because Lily asked, "So what do we do if we get inside and they try to split us up?"

"Tell them that you have to sit next to me in case I need my seizure medication," I replied matter-of-factly.

SMA does not cause seizures; I've never had one in my life, but toss out the word *seizure* next time you're trying to get something from a person of authority, and you'll be amazed at how understanding they become. To hammer the point home, I promised Lily that if she didn't do everything in her power to sit with me, I would tell the secret service that she was planning an assassination and have her removed from the venue. That's what friends are for.

While waiting in line to get in, secret service agents approached us and instructed "my companion" and me to follow them. We were with several friends, but we assumed this would eventually happen, so we didn't argue. Lily and I followed the badass dudes in suits around the side of the building and into the accessible entrance. Upon entering, we were greeted by an older man with a metal detection wand. At least I'm assuming that's what it was; maybe it was a Republican mentality detector, so that they could keep all opposition out of the rally. He scanned Lily and let her through, then surprisingly just waved me through the security checkpoint without checking me at all. I have a bag on the side of my chair that, for all he knew, could've been filled with bombs and knives and rocket launchers, but I'm a cute little wheelchair kid so obviously I can't be evil. I smiled and did my best to not look like a terrorist as I drove past him.

The gym was packed. A stage had been constructed on one end of the basketball court, and the rest of the floor was covered by thousands of human beings jamming themselves as close to the stage as possible. My initial thoughts were, "Holy shit. it's a thousand degrees in here," and "Where the hell am I supposed to sit?"

Off to the right I spotted a big blue handicap sign and some secret service agents standing around it. I moved toward the sign like a moth instinctively moves toward bright light.

A young woman with a volunteer sticker on her suit

jacket stood next to the handicap sign and explained to us that the disabled seating section was located in the front, near the stage. She led us down a narrow path created by a rope barrier along the edge of the gym.

When the handicap section came into view, my heart sank a little. It was a small area near the stage that was blocked off with rope and very noticeably overflowing with old people in wheelchairs. The volunteer lifted the rope for me and promptly closed it in front of Lily. Before I could maneuver my chair around to argue, another secret service agent was directing me into a spot to park my chair. I parked and waited. I can't turn my head or body very far in either direction, so when another wheelchair pulled up next to me, I was basically stuck staring straight ahead.

Someone off to my left, not in the handicap section, called my name multiple times, failing to understand that I physically couldn't turn my body to look at them. I felt bad, but this wasn't the first time this awkward situation had arisen, so I didn't let it get to me.

A text from Lily informed me that she was in the regular, standing-room-only section. The secret service would later let her into the handicap section, but she had to sit behind me, making communication impossible by any means other than text message.

I was pissed. But my annoyance only lasted for several minutes before I had the epiphany that I was really lucky to be seeing this speech at all. I had a great view of the stage and ultimately, it was not important if Lily was sitting next to me or behind me. We weren't at the speech to talk.

Fast forward a few hours, the speech was pretty good. Lots of "FOUR MORE YEARS!" chants, which were interesting. It was my first political rally, so I had nothing to compare it to. My mind was most captivated, however, by the people sitting around me in the handicap section. To my immediate left was a middle-aged woman in a manual wheelchair who spent a majority of the speech yelling, "DOWN IN FRONT!" attempting to make some people a few rows in front of us sit down. Assessing the position of her head, in relation to the position of Michelle on the stage, I decided she could see perfectly fine and was most likely just a curmudgeon. In front of me sat a very old man who read a very graphic war novel (I knew this because the font in his book was huge) the entire time Michelle spoke and kept adjusting his wheelchair to be farther to the left for no apparent reason. On my right sat two elderly war veterans, and I listened to them intently as they exchanged grim stories of racism back in the day. It was probably the most impactful moment of my night, hearing these two men discuss what it truly meant to have rights in America.

Then the speech ended. Raucous applause accompanied Michelle Obama as she walked off the stage and approached the handicap section. That's when things got nuts.

When the crowd realized that she was going to shake hands with the front row, everyone went completely ape shit.

The flimsy rope that blocked off the handicap section gave way as a flood of able-bodied people crashed into our area, pushing themselves between the wheelchairs to get to the front. The angry wheelchair woman to my left lost her mind and *jumped* out of her chair. I kid you not, she literally leaped out of that wheelchair, screamed Michelle's name repeatedly, climbed over an empty chair in front of her, and disappeared into the crowd that was surging toward the first lady.

This is when my fragility became a problem. Sitting in the middle of the handicap section, surrounded by wheelchairs, folding chairs, and crazed Obama supporters, I was suddenly very unsafe and very trapped. Large, heavy, adult bodies tripped over me and stumbled into me. I was merely an object for the fans to maneuver around. Generally people are abnormally careful around me, but on this night, if meeting Michelle meant smashing my body, I was getting smashed. All it would've taken is one stumbling person to connect with my head and my neck would've snapped like a twig.

To make matters worse, trying to forcibly drive my chair in any direction only caused more people to fall over me. All I could do was sit and hope that the craziness would subside and I would live to laugh about it later.

Eventually, Lily used her hulk strength to throw a few wheelchairs out of the way. She then lowered her shoulder and became my lead blocker as we barreled through the crowd on our way to the back door.

Overall, it was a very worthwhile experience. I didn't die, which is a plus! And let's be honest, if I had died in the chaos, it would've made an awesome story and the Obamas probably would've called my family to offer condolences, which is something not many people can say has happened to them.

chapter 28

the start of world domination

During my first few years of college, I grew out of the mind-set that my wheelchair was a huge social barrier and that little awkward interactions like needing to ask a stranger to lift my head up must be avoided at all costs to maintain my "normalcy" in the eyes of others. This shift in cognition—from trying to impress others by hiding or minimizing my disease, to accepting that SMA was a part of who I was and realizing that most people don't really care that I'm in a wheelchair—was a natural outcome of maturation. I believe this is one of the reasons that led me to start my blog.

On a boring day near the end of May after my freshman year of college, I had the random idea of starting a blog about my life.

Most of my friends were either still at college, or already on vacation, so I was spending the start of my summer doing a whole lot of nothing. On that boring day, while reclined in my wheelchair in the backyard—trying to get tan—I decided it might be fun to write a story about the time I fell out of my wheelchair and broke my femur. At first I was hesitant. Posting stories about my life on the Internet seemed conceited and egotistical. Also, my friends and I made fun of people who use their disability to gain attention, but that wasn't my intention.

I've always enjoyed making fun of the awkwardness, weirdness, and uniqueness of living with spinal muscular atrophy, but my audience was typically limited to my group of friends and my family. For some reason that I don't think I'll ever fully understand, I felt a sudden urge to make more people laugh at my disease.

As I began to type my broken femur story, it slowly dawned on me how much material I had to write about. I stopped writing to do a quick Google search for other blogs that were similar to what I was suddenly imagining in my head: a humorous take on a very serious disease. There were no results. The excitement started to build as I finished the femur story, wrote a brief introduction to my life, and posted both on my newly created Tumblr page: Laughing at My Nightmare!

At first nothing happened. I kept the blog a secret from my family and friends, mostly because I talked about dying in my first post—something I had never discussed with anyone out of fear that it would create permanent awkwardness in the way people thought about me. I also felt like I had a lot more freedom writing anonymously. Throughout June I privately messaged countless Tumblr users, asking them to check out my stories. I honestly just needed some validation for all the effort I had put into the stories that I had posted. Slowly, my number of followers started to climb. People began interacting with me, asking questions and telling me to write more.

> Anonymous asked:
> Have you ever considered getting an assistance animal, like a dog? Or has your family ever had any pets?
> Answer:
> I have an assistance turtle. He doesn't help much.

I reached my one thousandth follower on July 7, 2011. I couldn't believe what was happening. I had stopped messaging people long ago, which meant that people were now finding my blog on their own. Stories I wrote were making people laugh. Fan mail was clogging up my email faster than I could respond to it. It was nuts. One of my friends sent me a message on Facebook saying that he had found my blog on stumbleUpon.com and that he really enjoyed it. That's when I realized I was not going to be able to hide this from my friends and family much longer. I was still extremely nervous about telling them—my story topics now included sex, my questions about God, and more about my fear of dying—but I decided that any awkwardness that might result from me telling them was not worth the effort I was going through to keep it a secret. I could write only when no one was home. I didn't use any names in my stories, lest a reader make a connection and mention it to my family. For the same reason I couldn't post any photos (despite my burning desire to toss up some nudes, ladies).

Anonymous asked:
Is this for real?
Answer:
Nope. It's an elaborate hoax. I'm actually a 46-year-old female living in Bangladesh.

I told my brother about the blog a few days later and his response was, "If you need any pictures of my penis, just ask any girl at school." Excellent. That was Andrew's way of saying he supported me. I waited until the following week when we were on vacation in Ocean City, Maryland, to tell my parents. My heart pounded and my hands were sweating as I told them all about what I was doing at dinner on the boardwalk one night. They were more blown away by the several thousand followers I now had than concerned about the subject material I wrote about. No awkwardness at all. Their supportive reaction was such a relief that I posted my blog on my Facebook that night for my friends to see.

My blog was starting to take on a life of its own, growing exponentially. I was enjoying life more than I ever had before. Finally, I had discovered something I was good at, something that mattered. Being good at video games, getting good grades, and knowing lots about sports was cool, but I always lacked a particular skill that I loved enough to carry me toward the future with enthusiasm. In the first few months of my blog, I realized I was a writer, or at least that I loved writing so much that I wanted to become one someday.

> Anonymous asked:
> How did you get your disease? :(
> Answer:
> I was bitten by someone else who had it.

By August, several newspapers and online news web sites had even contacted me about doing stories. Everything started to feel unbelievable. Three months prior I had posted a dumb little story about breaking my femur, and now people wanted to write stories about me?

My blog was a source for entertainment, but I realized I had the opportunity to make a real impact on the world. In January, I started a nonprofit organization, called Laughing at My Nightmare, Inc., with a group of awesome individuals.

Our mission was to encourage individuals to remain positive in the face of adversity through the use of humor, while also supporting muscular dystrophy research.

The idea for Laughing at My Nightmare, Inc., came from the readers of my blog, and a series of conversations I had with my cousin, Sarah Burcaw (Becca's older sister). Sarah transferred to Moravian during my sophomore year, just as the blog was starting to skyrocket. We ate lunch together, and the hot topic of discussion was usually the craziness of my blog's popularity. We scrolled through the abundance of emails I was getting from all over the world and marveled at how honest complete strangers were being with me. A man from New Mexico wrote to tell me that he was contemplating suicide when he found my blog. Its message of using humor to cope with adversity, he said, kept him from putting his thoughts into action that night. A man recounted his life of cross-dressing to me in a lengthy email, detailing moments of intense anguish and hopelessness. He said my blog made him see life in a completely new way. He was going to start letting go of the anger he kept inside him from the prejudice he faced, and focus on living more positively. A teenage girl with cancer told me that my stories were helping her laugh amid the torture of chemo. Laughing just felt so good, she said.

That's really where the idea originated. Sarah and I read hundreds of those emails in awe, and began to see that laughter wasn't just fun, it was needed. How could we take that message and put it out there for even more people to grab hold of? Both of us were big dreamers. What if we opened up a comedy club? Probably too expensive. An amusement park? Where would we put it, my backyard? What if we traveled to schools and talked about humor and positivity? Yes. Holy crap that sounded awesome! We could help kids see that life was what they made it.

What if we created a nonprofit to spread this idea? Bingo.

Raising money for muscular dystrophy research, we agreed, was also a perfect cause for us to financially support. There was a moment of pure exhilaration when I realized Sarah and I were in this together.

Founders of Laughing at My Nightmare, Inc.

In fifth grade I wanted to start my own comic book series. The idea died when my best friends lost enthusiasm after the first issue. Too much work. In sixth grade I tried to start a skateboarding team, but nobody wanted to practice. They just wanted to design a logo and tell people they were on a skate team. In eighth grade Pat and Andrew and I set up a lemonade stand (way too old, I know) and made $132 in one day. The next morning I pleaded with them to set up the stand for one more day. We could have done it every day and been millionaires by the end of summer. Too much work, not enough fun. Let's just go spend the money, they said. I felt like all of my grand ideas throughout life had been squandered by the laziness of friends. When we decided to start a nonprofit, Sarah was a ball of fiery enthusiasm, and her commitment excited me more than the idea itself.

Eventually we began a six-month process of meeting with lawyers and business advisors, working hours every day to formulate our brand and the activities we would do, and filling out more paperwork than I ever want to think about again. But on that first day, as our nonprofit baby was birthed, we wanted to accomplish something to make it seem real.

We decided to sell something with our name on it. Not only would they raise some start-up funds, but it would spread awareness: Marketing 101. Sarah pulled out her laptop and credit card. We googled "bulk wristbands," clicked the first web site that came up, designed a cheap, but fashionable purple wristband (which turned out to be pink when they arrived, but that's what you get for eight-cent wristbands), and that night I set up a free Web store and promoted it on my blog and social media. I fell asleep to wild thoughts of waking up with a few dozen orders.

Eighty-three orders in the first night. Eighty-three. Everywhere from Bangkok to Sydney to London to Los Angeles, the wristbands were a huge success. We sold out of our first thousand in just a few days, confirming that the world supported our idea.

I continued to write stories as often as possible throughout the spring semester. My followers climbed over fifty thousand, and our nonprofit had its first official board meeting. Over the next year, my followers continued to rise up over five hundred thousand. I filmed several documentaries about my life and the nonprofit. I spoke at countless schools and met some incredible people.

Another interesting outcome of all this craziness was the discovery that blogging can, in fact, lead to ladies.

chapter 29

first (real) girlfriend

"Hey, Shane, I know this is going to seem weird, but I added your brother on Facebook and asked him for your number because I've been reading your blog for a long time and I just really want to get to know you. If you're totally creeped out I understand, you don't have to text me back, but I would love to talk to you!"

This is the text message that I woke up to on a painfully cold October morning in my sophomore year of college. Having just been yanked from the perfect warmth of my bed and forced to suffer through the inhumane torture of showering at 6 a.m., I was not in any state of mind to deal with formulating a reaction to what I read, let alone try to type out a response. So I put my phone away without giving the text a second thought and returned to huddling over my cup of steaming coffee. I've never been a morning person.

An hour later, I was sitting in my Research Methods of Psychology class. My body was now awake and functioning, but my brain was still getting dressed and brushing its teeth. Staring at my lap, pretending to listen to my professor, but mostly just trying not to let my eyes close, I thought about the insanity of the last few months. What started as a random attempt to make people laugh had transformed into a blog that was attracting thousands of readers every day. *What was going on?*

Around lunchtime, I remembered the mysterious text I'd read earlier that morning and brought it up on my phone to reread.

Oh God, another crazy follower, was my first thought. At this point, my blog was beginning to take off at a dizzying rate. I was getting at least a few dozen emails a day, and many of them were along the lines of "OMG. I LOVE YOU. OMG." I genuinely appreciated every email, but quite honestly, I was starting to become numb to the messages. These people liked the words I wrote, they were not actually in love with me. However, this was the first time a follower had gone through the effort of finding my cell phone number to text me fan mail. I respect a dedicated effort. For that reason I decided to humor this anonymous person, and I sent back a text that read, "Hahaha hey! What's up?" *This is so weird. This is so weird. This is so weird.*

After getting past the awkwardness of texting a complete stranger, I learned that her name was Jill, she was twenty-two, and she lived only about an hour away from me. By the evening, after we'd been texting most of the day, I became aware of my heart beating just a little harder every time my phone buzzed and her name came up on the screen. The conversation slowly transitioned from casual to intense. Inevitably, the subject of significant others was brought up, and at first I felt uneasy and annoyed that our chat was progressing in that direction. Relationships were a sore subject. I still hadn't had one. At the same time, I couldn't help but feel intrigued. She was the one to bring up the issue. In my limited experience, I always had to be the one to start this conversation, since girls are generally not interested in me. The few times I tried throughout my life, bringing up the topic in a nonchalant manner (so they didn't get scared away by the wheelchair kid making subtle hints at more than friendship), it always felt like I was being a douche bag. *Girls don't want to date you*, I told myself; talking about relationships and being flirty was pointless. Nonetheless, she asked me if I had a girlfriend. Battling nervous excitement, I decided to test the waters. *Fuck it, if she gets turned off and runs away, I will stop texting back and move on with my life as if she never existed* (not proud of that thought).

Explaining my lack of relationship experience is about as much fun as having a cavity drilled (I've never had a cavity): *Hey, I've never had a girlfriend, and I have a sneaking suspicion that it has to do with my disease. Why, you ask? Well, for one, there are the 9000 things I need help with/can't do, which seems to be a turn off for most girls, since I've been friend zoned more times than I can count.*

Her response was simple, but it turned my heart upside down and made my palms sweat: "I don't need physical intimacy from a relationship, because that's not what is important to me. With that being said, I would enjoy being physical with you, and I don't see any reason why we couldn't be. You said yourself on your blog that everything works. We might have to do things differently, but I like different."

Mind blown. This wasn't happening. I had only "met" her a few hours ago, and that was only via text message after she had, for all intents and purposes, stalked me to find my phone number. She could be a forty-seven-year-old man for all I knew. Throwing these cautions to the wind, I flirted back, saying something about the irony of how my equipment works just fine despite how shitty the rest of my body is. I didn't sleep that night.

We continued talking first thing the next day, and a few days later we Skyped for the first time. (She was not a forty-seven-year-old man, but in fact, a pretty twenty-two-year-old girl.) Our conversations over the next few weeks confirmed that we were both very interested in each other, as the topics ranged from our mutual affection for music, to the logistics of how she was going to give me the greatest (and first) blow job I'd ever gotten. I was in awe of her willingness to be sexual with me. I was blinded by the sexuality. I never once stopped to consider how fast things were progressing. I blame my hormones. Skype and texting quickly became insufficient means for sharing our affection. We started planning her first visit. That semester, I had classes only on Tuesdays and Thursdays, which meant that I was home alone for most of every Monday, Wednesday, and Friday. A Friday was selected so that we could be alone together for a large portion of the day. I told my parents I was having a "friend" over, who I had met through the blog. They were very unsettled about letting a stranger come over while I was home alone, but I guess I was a good whiner because they eventually gave in.

Fast forward a few weeks.

The front door opened and my heart nearly leaped out of my chest to greet Jill for the first time. It was early in the morning, probably not even 10 a.m. Well before the appropriate time to begin hanging out with someone, but we didn't care. A month of constant Skyping had built up so much tension that seeing her walk through the door practically made me fall out of my wheelchair.

"I love you," were the first words to come out of my mouth, thinking I was being suave. Instant regret. My face got red and started to burn when I heard her utter the same phrase in response. *You don't love her*, danced around inside my head for a few seconds before I shut the thought out while making small talk about traffic and coffee and being tired and other boring topics that neither of us cared about. She sat on the couch close to where I sat in my wheelchair, probably noticing my eyes wander up and down her body. I still remember the black sweater and skirt she wore. We had previously agreed that it would be a "lazy day" of watching movies, and that we were not going to dress nicely for each other. It relieved the tension of meeting in person for the first time. Apparently, neither of us had chosen to abide by the dress code of sweatpants and T-shirts, though.

After talking for a while, we decided to move to my bedroom and commence the planned activities for lazy day: laying in bed together watching movies on Netflix. She sat down on the edge of my bed and told me to come closer. *Welp, here goes nothing!* A lifetime of fearing that I would never experience real physical contact with a girl, an intense fear that I was unprepared for being intimate, and a very realistic fear that one of my parents would come home and find us, were all shoved into the back of my mind as I positioned my chair so that our faces were only inches away from each other. It was 11 a.m. and Mom would undoubtedly be stopping home for lunch around 12:15 to meet Jill (and to make sure we weren't being naughty), but I ignored that thought, too.

We looked into each other's eyes as she gently put her hands on my neck, supporting the back of my head in such a natural way, and leaned into me. I closed my eyes and stopped thinking for perhaps the first time in my life as our lips met. We breathed hard as little sighs of exhilaration escaped our mouths' in between kisses. I slipped my tongue inside her mouth and let it wrestle hers. She giggled and did the same. Several times we got so into it that I lost balance of my head and it went flopping back into that terribly uncomfortable position. One of the times it fell she refused to help me up and continued kissing my neck. I could not have been happier.

"All right, do you want to try to lift me out of my chair?" I asked her, the nerves returning full force.

"Yes," she chirped before kissing me several more times.

I backed away from her embrace and prepared myself for teaching a new person how to lift me.

In bed we snuggled up close to each other, which was harder than you might imagine. At first we tried sharing a pillow, but when she slid close to my body and rested her head next to mine, my entire body tipped toward the slight incline in the mattress that she created by lying next to me. My face smashed up against hers and my knees rested against her thighs. Not exactly romantic. We giggled like two stupid kids and continued kissing while trying to rearrange our bodies into a position that allowed us to be close, but also comfortable. Eventually we found a spot on the bed that worked nicely. Both of us were kind of halfway on our sides, facing each other, and we used an extra pillow to prop my head into the perfect making-out position.

Once again I lost control of my mind. Having a real human girl to share this kind of intimacy with was surreal. After eighteen years of believing I would never find someone who didn't care about my disease, my tiny arms, my weak muscles, my wheelchair, my dependency on others, my inevitable decline, my death, and now here lay Jill, caressing me and kissing me and acting like I was the sexiest, most able-bodied boy she had ever met.

Then, to my surprise, Jill started sliding her hand down the front of my pants. Holy shit. This was happening.

Let's stop the story for a minute so I can explain some background. It's getting kind of steamy, anyway.

My penis works fine. Erections are the result of an avalanche of blood rushing into the penile cavity (that's the medical definition, anyway). SMA doesn't affect my blood avalanche capabilities, so I get boners and keep them just as well as any horse (I mean person).

"Can you masturbate?" is a question I get asked at least once a day by anonymous people reading my blog. Weird thing to ask, by the way. But the answer is that I used to be able to. Before my wrists and elbows became too weak and atrophied to reach down between my legs while lying on my back in bed, I had no trouble partaking in that form of entertainment. Of course I had to be smart about it, since the clean up process could be a little tricky. My solution was to lie in bed to "watch a movie." Then I would tell someone in my family that I had a runny nose, asking for a few tissues to hold while I "watched the movie." After unloading into the handful of tissues, I'd wrap them into a neat little pile that hid the contents very nicely. Besides, when I asked someone to throw away a handful of "snot-" drenched tissues, their natural reaction was to grab more tissues to separate their hands from the slimeball as much as possible. (Have you puked yet? I feel no regret. You gotta do what you gotta do!)

Eventually, I lost the physical ability in my arms to masturbate. It sucked. There's no pretty way to put it. It just plain sucked. I started having wet dreams all the time, which meant waking up and deciding between lying in a puddle of my own semen for the rest of life or calling my dad to help me get cleaned up.

As you can see there was more than one reason why Jill's hand sliding down my pants excited me. I practically lost it the instant her hand slipped under the waistband of my boxers. But for the sake of being cool and macho or something stupid like that I held it together.

To all my family finding this out for the first time, especially you Mom and Dad, um, don't be mad. I love you a lot. Next time we see each other let's just pretend you didn't read this chapter.

Jill proceeded to take my pants off. We snuggled closer under my blankets and she gave me the best orgasm I had ever experienced to that point in my life. It took me a solid few minutes to regain mental function. When I did return to earth, my responsible side took over. It was almost noon, and my mom would be home soon. We were both half naked and not in any mood to get out of bed. However, it takes an expert caregiver (like my parents or brother) about ten minutes to get me dressed and in my chair, and that's when I'm NOT a mess. Panic set in and propelled us to clean up as quickly as humanly possible. By "we" I mean "she." I basically just lay there offering moral support in between bouts of laughter at the absurdity of the situation.

We flew through a crash course in getting Shane dressed and were able to get ourselves into the dining room just as my mom came through the front door.

After I introduced Jill, Mom asked, "So, what have you two been up to?"

"Not much, just hanging out," I said, glancing at Jill with a subtle wink. Mission accomplished.

Once Mom left again we went right back to our previous activities. It was an exhausting day, but it left me with an incredible sense of hope. Jill was clearly very into me.

Living an hour away and both being in school meant we couldn't hang out as often as we liked. The texting and Skyping were constant, but it just didn't compare to the physical intimacy we could share when we were together. A few weeks later I asked her to be my girlfriend, feeling like it was the natural progression of our relationship, considering how sexual we were being every time she visited, and how much I liked her. She agreed and I crossed another "never have I ever" off my list. It was a huge moment.

Jill and I were very happy together for a few months. We hung out as often as our schedules allowed, went on dates, had "sexy time" whenever possible, and learned a lot about each other. But somewhere along the way, my feelings started to change. I noticed myself feeling like I wasn't as emotionally invested as I should have been. During some soul searching, it occurred to me that I had gotten so wrapped up in finding a girl who was interested in being sexual with me that I had forgotten the values that truly matter in a relationship. I had ignored vital aspects of growing closer to Jill while focusing on the intimacy. I suddenly felt like I was only interested because of the amazing orgasms I was getting. Those feelings, coupled with increasing responsibilities in other areas of my life, led me to decide that it wasn't fair of me to stay with Jill. I could have easily lied and pretended I felt more than physical attraction, but it never would have worked out and deep down I knew I couldn't do that to her.

We stopped speaking after I ended it. Maybe it's fucked up that I'm saying all this in my book, but Jill really did change my life. She helped me defeat the false idea I had held on to so tightly that having a girlfriend was impossible. She taught me that there are people out there who really will see past the wheelchair and want to be with me despite the difficulties of dating someone with SMA. I can never thank her enough for our time together and everything I took away from it.

chapter 30

physical therapy (read: torture)

Since physical therapy can help slow the effects of muscle atrophy, I've been getting physical therapy on a regular basis since I was a baby. The concept of how it helps me isn't something I've ever really thought about or tried to explain to someone; it's just a part of my life. I realize that it might be slightly confusing to understand, so before I start with the funny stories, I'll try to explain how physical therapy works for me.

A long time ago, when I was in early elementary school, my wrists looked completely normal. They were straight and I could bend them in all the normal directions. Now, I can't straighten them much past the ninety-degree angle that they're fixed at in the picture below, and if someone helps me extend them, they still only straighten to about a 110 degrees.

Observe.

In physical therapy, my therapist stretches out all of my muscles so that the atrophying process progresses at a slower rate than if I didn't receive physical therapy. Think about it, when you sit in one position for a long period of time and then stand up, your leg muscles feel a little sore, right? The muscles in my body remain in relatively the same position all day every day, which is why they atrophy. My disease causes my muscles to deteriorate and weaken, and since I never move, they get stuck in the position that they're in all day. Physical therapy serves the same purpose as standing up after you've been sitting for a long time; it stretches my muscles out.

For people with SMA, physical therapy consists of prolonged stretches of all the limbs. My therapist will push my wrists, or my knees, or my ankles, as far in the correct position as possible and hold them there for several minutes. The simple truth is that I'm sitting in my wheelchair a hell of a lot more of the time than I spend at physical therapy, so by a matter of the demands of daily life my muscles get more atrophied over time. This means that, today, my physical therapist can push my wrist to a 110 degrees, but my muscles stop straightening at a certain point and go no further unless they tear, strain, or sprain. It's kind of a losing battle when you think about it, but after I spend an hour in physical therapy I feel substantially looser, which is a great feeling. Also, imagine how fast my muscles would atrophy if I didn't receive physical therapy on a regular basis, so there are definitely some benefits as well.

From my toddler years until about third or fourth grade, I received physical therapy from a woman my family knew who had a private practice out of her home. She basically only treated kids with some type of disability, so she really knew what she was doing despite the fact that therapy took place on her living room floor. Around that time I also used a device we called The Stander that simulated standing. It was hell.

I absolutely hated physical therapy in the worst way during these years of my life. The shitty part about stretching out an atrophied muscle is that it hurts, and like I said before, if you stretch it too far, there can be serious physical injuries that result.

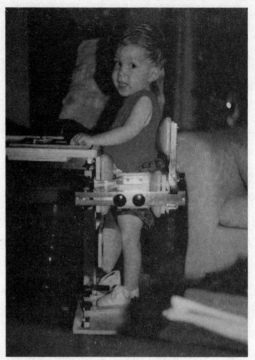

Take the fucking picture so I can lie down.

However, I was also kind of a baby when it came to pain back in those days. Growing up, I was shielded from pain by my wheelchair and the fact that I didn't do much physical stuff that could put me in danger of getting hurt, so I didn't learn how to tolerate pain as fast as normal kids do. Although my naïve brain exaggerated the pain, it still hurt, and I wasn't old enough to appreciate that my physical therapist was actually doing a world of good for my body by stretching it out. I received therapy only once a week back then, but whenever that day rolled around, I would get all panicky and try to find ways to get out of going. Sometimes I would wait until my mom said it was time to go, and then I would pretend like I really needed to use the bathroom all of a sudden to waste a few minutes.

During those early therapy days, I developed a hypersensitivity to pain. I would anticipate a stretch hurting before my therapist had even started the stretch, and I would inevitably start yelling, "OW, OW, OW, OW!" The problem then became that my therapist didn't know when I was anticipating pain or actually feeling pain, and because of this I experienced some of my first muscle sprains during this time.

I want to try for one second to convey how terrifying it is to have absolutely no power over the muscles in my body while they're being stretched. If you were at physical therapy, and you felt like a stretch was going too far, you could easily tighten your muscle, stopping the stretch and avoiding the pain. I can't do that. I have to rely on verbal communication and trust that my physical therapist will listen to me when I say that a stretch is going too far and that I'm about to get hurt, but sometimes verbal communication just isn't enough.

When I was in middle school, I started receiving physical therapy at a rehab facility that is associated with the main hospital in my town. They have a whole pediatric division of the facility, where they mostly treat kids with disabilities. For my first few years at this facility, the same guy treated me each week, and to this day he is my least favorite physical therapist of all time.

This guy, we'll call him Brett, was in my opinion the absolute worst kind of physical therapist, which is kind of ironic because the stories he told indicated that he was a big shot in the world of physical therapy; although, I later found out that many people believed that Brett was a compulsive liar. He was the kind of guy who would complain about having to fly down to his beach house for a weekend to meet the maintenance man. Anyway, Brett gave less than half a shit about the opinions of his patients. He was a middle-aged man who acted like he'd been sent to Earth by God himself to perform physical therapy on the less fortunate. He may have been a great physical therapist for most other people, but he just refused to understand that my muscles could not withstand the same amount of pressure as everybody else's. I think it was his secret goal to completely straighten all of my muscles, even though that was physically impossible by the time I started seeing him.

There is one incident that took place as a result of Brett's power complex that sticks out in my mind as the worst physical therapy experience I've ever had. I was probably fourteen or fifteen years old and it was an evaluation night, which was something the physical therapists did four times a year for each patient to measure if any progress was being made. This system makes no sense for someone with a disease that gets progressively worse; I'm obviously never going to make progress, but that's beside the point. During an evaluation, Brett had to use a protractor-type device to measure the maximum angle that all my muscles could be stretched to. Brett fucking loved evaluations; I lost sleep worrying about them whenever one was approaching.

My knees have always been the most severely affected part of my body, since they move the least on a day-to-day basis. So in the typical "do exactly opposite of what Shane wants" Brett fashion, he stretched my knees the most aggressively of all my other muscles. I will give him this much credit, *most* of the time when Brett was stretching my knees and I began to wince, he would back off so I didn't get hurt. By the age of fourteen, I had developed a much higher pain tolerance and didn't cry wolf every time I thought a stretch was going to hurt. However, I always felt like Brett kind of doubted if I was ever in real pain when I yelped during a stretch, and I yelped only when I felt legitimate pain, so you can understand my constant underlying distrust of him.

On this particular evaluation night, Brett boasted that we were going to set a record for my knees by performing a prolonged, gentle stretch, as opposed to a short, aggressive one. I felt sick at the thought of straightening my knee more than it has ever been straightened, but slow, long stretches were usually less painful, so I didn't argue with him. My hands started to sweat buckets as he began to stretch my left knee. As the minutes ticked by, I lay on the therapy table and concentrated on trying to relax my muscles, which is pretty much physically impossible, but something I like to mentally tell myself I'm doing to stop a stretch from hurting. I remember looking out the tiny window in the corner of the small room we were in and noticing that it was considerably dark for 5 p.m. It was winter, and I remember having a brief thought that it might snow and that school would be canceled. I forgot what was going on for a split second at the thought of a snow day. Then he started to stretch my knee too far.

I could feel my muscle reaching its maximum stretching point, the point where I know if the therapist continues to stretch it any further, something is going to give and I'm going to get hurt.

"Oh God! Okay, no further, no further. It hurts!" I said in a hurried voice to get him to stop.

"Just a little longer, we're almost there," replied Brett nonchalantly, as he continued to push down on my knee.

These were the exact words I didn't want to hear him say because I knew no matter what I said there was no stopping him from going further. He pushed even harder on my knee and I began to quietly whimper, "Oh God, oh God, oh God!" I hated him so much.

"NO SERIOUSLY, IT REALLY HURTS! PLEASE STOP!" I yelled.

Then it happened. A bolt of lightning exploded in my hamstring and shot all the way up my leg and throughout the rest of my body. Almost as if in slow motion, I could feel the fibers in my hamstring pulling apart from each other. They made a sound like sandpaper on wood that I could hear and feel on the inside of my body. The most intense burning pain I've ever felt flooded my entire knee, and I screamed at the same time that my knee muscles gave way and straightened further than they had ever straightened in my life. Brett obviously was terrified by this and let go of my leg immediately; he had not intended for my leg to straighten this far. He frantically started apologizing, but by that point the pain was so unbearable that my uncontrollable sobbing and my dad's efforts to put my leg back to its natural position forced Brett into the background. I was a complete mess.

Probably a half hour later, with two people stabilizing my leg, my dad was able to lift me back into my chair so we could go home. It is a good thing that Brett didn't try to talk to me before I left, because I would have ruined the rest of his life in a matter of a few sentences, my anger toward him was worse than the pain.

My knee didn't heal for several months, probably because I refused to go to the hospital, arguing that it was only sprained, when in reality Brett had probably either partially or completely torn my hamstring. It was close to a year before I could stretch that leg without any pain. Brett found a new job in a different state several weeks after the incident, which was most likely just a coincidence, but I like to think he quit because of me.

Another time, I was receiving physical therapy in high school, through our school district's physical therapy program. It was 7:30 in the morning, and I was being stretched before school started on a table in the back of the nurse's office at my high school. When therapy was over my therapist had to lift me off the table and put me back in my chair, however, in a way that I still don't understand, my left arm got caught on my therapist's shirt and twisted in an odd direction while he was spinning me into the correct position to get in my wheelchair. All of a sudden, incredible pain filled my upper left arm, absolutely incredible. It kind of caught me off guard and I yelled a bunch of nonintelligible words along the lines of, "Holyshitthathurtsstophelpohmygodowowowow."

My therapist put me back in my wheelchair and although I was almost hyperventilating from the pain, the severity of the situation didn't set in until I tried and failed to move my left arm. Nothing. Here's the funny part: I once again convinced everyone that it was only sprained, out of my pure desire to stay as far away from hospitals as possible, and I suffered through close to two months of torturous pain every time I had to allow my parents to move my arm to change my shirt each day.

A few months later, once my arm was feeling better, I went down to duPont Hospital in Delaware for a checkup with my doctors. One of them wanted me to have an X-ray on my ribs to check out my lungs, and while he was examining my X-ray he noticed that I had fractured my left arm and that it had healed on its own. Whoops!

Now that I think about it, most of the stories I have about me getting hurt are when I've been in physical therapy. Maybe someone needs to reevaluate the effectiveness and dangers of stretching kids with SMA.

chapter 31

whip my dick out

When you rely on other people to help you do mostly everything, there are inevitably going to be some embarrassing situations that arise.

One day in the summer of my sophomore year of college, I went to Becca's house to chill for the afternoon, while my brother went swimming at his friend's house. Becca and I sat outside all afternoon getting tan, and I drank a can of Pepsi when it started to get unbearably hot. Around three in the afternoon I realized I wasn't going to be able to stay at Becca's house much longer because I really needed to pee. The cup of coffee I had when I woke up, combined with the can of Pepsi, was finding its way to the end of my bladder.

Going to the bathroom is a relatively complicated process for me. This is how it used to work: someone gets me out of my chair, lays me down on a flat surface on my back, I whip my dick out, and relieve myself in the pee jar. Unfortunately, in the past couple of years, I've lost arm strength and range of motion so the process has changed slightly and involves the person having to "steer me in the right direction" using the opening of the jar.

My brother met me at Becca's house on his way home from swimming and we started walking back to our house so I could pee. However, we decided to stop at Arby's on the way because my intense urge for loaded potato bites outweighed my need to urinate. I stupidly drank a Dr Pepper with my potato bites. I was so healthy.

We arrived at our house and I wheelchair-sprinted into my bedroom, yelling at Andrew to hurry. A few years earlier, Andrew and I got over the awkwardness barrier of him helping me pee. We found a method where he doesn't have to look at or touch anything, and having someone else, besides my parents, be able to help me go to the bathroom gave me a lot more freedom. To streamline the process, Andrew and I came up with a group of words we used to instruct each other when he helped me pee.

Usually, the person helping me keeps a hand on the handle of the pee jar while I pee to ensure that nothing crazy happens and I don't pee all over the bed. Andrew got me all lined up and walked away to change the song that was playing on his laptop in the other room.

Here's how our conversation went:

"Uhh, dude, hold this?"

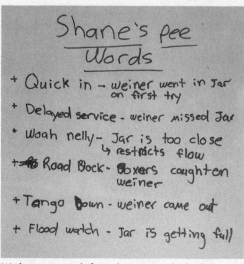

We have too much fun taking me to the bathroom.

"You'll be fine, just go."

"I don't want the jar to tip. Just hold it!"

"You'll be fine."

So I peed. A lot. It was one of those glorious moments when everything important in life faded into nothing and all of my existence became focused on the amazing feeling of my bladder shrinking.

Suddenly, the jar became too full, and just as I had expected, started to tip.

"Dude, it's tipping!"

"What?"

"THE JAR IS TIPPING! COME HERE!"

But it was too late. The opening of the jar had passed the point of no return and a disgusting amount of warm piss was running down my thigh, forming a steamy puddle beneath my hips. My brother ran in and immediately doubled over from laughter. I began laughing, too, pretty much uncontrollably. I was lying in a puddle of my own urine.

Then it got gross, and while we continued to laugh uncontrollably I had to quickly tell him to go get towels to start cleaning everything up. I obviously had to change my boxers and shorts, but somehow my shirt got wet, too.

I also ruined my memory-foam mattress. Fuck.

A Conversation with Mom

Mom: Shane, you need to remember to watch what you say on your blog.

Me: Uh, what?

Mom: Like, your wiener words.

chapter 32

feeding tube drama

Before writing this chapter, I asked my dad to
weigh me. To do this, he picks me up like a sack of potatoes
and stands on the scale with me in his arms. It's kind of
romantic. Once he has that weight, he puts me back in my
chair and weighs himself alone. I make fun of him for being
fat, and then he does some kind of weird calculus equation
using the two weights to figure out how much I weigh. Science is pretty neat, huh?

Seven minutes before writing this chapter, on August 14,
2013, I, Shane Robert Burcaw, weigh a whopping sixty-five
pounds. Believe it or not, I'm actually excited that I have
gained a few pounds since the last time I was weighed. My
weight has been somewhat of a roller coaster over the past
few years, the kind of roller coaster where you get really close
to almost dying because you don't weigh enough.

At my lowest, I weighed forty-six pounds. A doctor told me I was going to die if I didn't get a feeding tube to gain some weight, and a several-year journey to accomplish that began.

Today, before I go to bed every night my dad sticks a long, yellow, rubbery feeding tube up my nostril. I swallow and occasionally gag until it goes down into my stomach. We secure the end that's left sticking out of my face to my cheek with a Band-Aid and attach it to a feeding tube pump, which blasts pure calories into my stomach while I sleep.

> Whenever my dad and I get into a fake argument, he always whips out the "Well, have fun getting into bed tonight," and I feel like that's kinda cheating.

When I wake up in the morning, my dad pulls off the Band-Aid and pulls the feeding tube out of me like he's starting a lawn mower. For a few hours I feel bloated and disgusting, but not so bad that I don't repeat the process again and again every single night. This routine is abnormal, even by SMA/feeding tube standards. When kids need feeding tubes, they usually have a surgery to have a permanent little valve created in their stomach.

I volunteered to do the feeding tube my way for a number of reasons, not only because nasal stimulation gives me a huge boner.

The decline began back in eleventh grade when I broke my femur and had to stay in that hospital bed for a month. I couldn't eat very well during that month, and although we tried everything from mashed potatoes to a ground up Mc-Double, I lost some weight during those obnoxious weeks while I was stuck in bed. I might have gained some weight back once I was recovered, but then in my senior year of high school, I got sick during Thanksgiving break and remained sick straight through until Christmas. A few days after Christmas I gave in and allowed my parents to take me to the hospital because I pretty much couldn't breathe. I was admitted with pneumonia, but once again God/Luck/Fate/Science/Life was on my side and I got better and was released four days later. Unfortunately, I lost eight or nine more pounds during this time, taking me down to about forty-seven pounds. Not good.

When I went to my yearly checkup that spring at DuPont Hospital, my doctors were not at all happy with my weight. One of my doctors showed me a graph of my weight distributed over time, speaking to me like a child and explaining that the sudden drop off in weight was not a good thing. "What do you think we need to do about this?" she said in a patronizing voice that made me want to throw myself out of my chair.

"I don't know, I'll just try more to eat more I guess," I desperately said, as I began to feel the tears welling up in my eyes; I knew what was coming next.

"I think it's time we think about a feeding tube. You're

going to need one eventually. We need to do the surgery while you're healthy, before it's too late." The condescending tone of her voice made this statement about a thousand times worse.

I never openly cried in front of other people, but it felt like my whole life was crashing down on top of me. Everything was happening too fast; I was about to graduate high school. The last thing I needed was a huge, life-changing surgery that would effectively change the way I had to live. My doctors and the interns that follow the doctors into every room stood there in silent, awkward disbelief and watched as I put my head down and let the flow of tears fall onto my lap. The thought of having a hole in my stomach and being attached to a bag of nutritional formula every night was the ultimate symbol of losing the fight against my disease, at least in my mind. I couldn't formulate a single rational thought, all I could think was "No, I don't need a feeding tube, not yet."

I felt pathetic, and there was a really hot intern in the room, which made it all the more embarrassing. Almost immediately I made a decision that crying and bitching was not going to get me anywhere, and as badly as I wanted to scream and never return to that hospital ever again, I calmed myself and listened to the doctors as they explained the feeding tube procedure and what we had to do to get it scheduled before I started college.

We scheduled the surgery for the middle of the summer. Meanwhile, I tried to gain weight on my own, reasoning that if I could show my doctors that I could get fat by myself, I could delay the surgery awhile longer. I found these super-caloric milkshake mixes called ScandiShakes that could only be ordered online for a very expensive price. My family and friends generously rallied behind this idea of mine and helped my parents purchase a bunch of cases. I started drinking two of these eight-hundred-calorie milkshakes a day. Scandi-Shakes are extremely thick and made me want to kill myself every time I finished one, but they are also pretty legit; I gained about three pounds using these shakes, but to my dismay, it was not enough weight to put off the feeding tube.

People asked me why I didn't just eat more. I wish it were that easy. At this point, I was getting tired after only a few minutes of chewing. I had to use actual energy to chew, so when I ate, my body was burning calories faster than I could shovel it in. I began to accept that the ScandiShakes were not going to be a miracle solution, and after having some discussions with my friends and family, I came to peace with the fact that a feeding tube was in my best interest.

But I wasn't excited about it by any means. In my mind, getting a feeding tube would greatly diminish my freedom to do what I wanted, because I would be forced to adopt some type of overnight feeding schedule when I would be hooked to the feeding machine. I also had this warped idea that I sort of looked like a normal person and that a tube sticking out of my stomach was going to turn me into someone that totally repulsed other people.

Remember that camp for kids with muscular dystrophy from when I was in the sixth grade? One of the kids in my cabin had a feeding tube, and back then, it scared the shit out of me. While we were sleeping one night, I was woken up by some of the counselors in our cabin making a fuss around this kid's bed. I looked over, and to my horror, his stomach juices were leaking out of the feeding tube. Somehow his tube had come disconnected from the machine and formula and stomach acid were pouring out onto the bed. I'm pretty sure I have some deep-rooted scarring from that incident.

So I had that pleasant memory to contemplate during the hour-long drive down to DuPont Hospital the day before the surgery was scheduled to take place. At this point, I just wanted to get the surgery done with so I could return to enjoying my summer. My friends and family convinced me that while it would be different, a tube sticking out of my stomach was not going to ruin my entire life.

My dad and I arrived at the hospital and made our way to the presurgical ward where I was scheduled to meet the surgeon that would be doing the operation. First, an anesthesiologist came into the room and told us she would be in charge of putting me to sleep and monitoring my condition during the operation. Then she said that there were some very serious issues we had to discuss before deciding to go through with the procedure. My dad and I both looked at each other with the same "What the hell is she talking about?" expression on our faces. We were under the impression that this surgery was no big deal and that these little presurgical meetings were just a formality.

The anesthesiologist, who had the bedside manner of a dead cow, told me in a very solemn tone that they would have to put a breathing tube down my throat to keep me alive during the surgery, and because of my weak lung muscles, there was a very real chance that when they tried to remove the breathing tube after the operation, my lungs would collapse and essentially I would die. It was such a slap in the face that I almost wanted to argue with her and tell her that I would be fine, but she just continued by telling me that if they felt my lungs would not be able to support themselves, they might have to leave the breathing tube in, "for an extended period of time or even permanently."

Seriously, what the fuck? I already had made plans for the day after my surgery, because the doctors that urged me to get it made it seem like it everybody and her sister got feeding tubes and it was no big deal. Now, another doctor was telling me that there was a good chance I would either die or become dependent on life support during this surgery. She ended by telling us that we needed to go home and strongly weigh our options before deciding what we wanted to do. My dad, beginning to get angry by her lack of human emotions, told her that the surgery was already scheduled for tomorrow and questioned why we were not told this information much sooner. Her response was basically a reiteration of her original point as well as hinting that the right decision was to not do the surgery.

We sat there in disbelief and confusion as the anesthesiologist left and the surgeon walked into the room. The surgeon was much cooler, and I liked him as a person right off the bat. He kind of joked around about the anesthesiologist being creepy with us, which made me feel much better about the entire ordeal. My dad put me on the examination table, and the surgeon started poking around my stomach and ribs, while explaining to us how he was planning to do the surgery. Out of nowhere he became very serious and told us that because of the way my body was shaped and the position of my stomach, there was a chance that they would not be able to place the feeding tube correctly. He went on to say that while the anesthesiologist might have been unpleasant about the situation, she was correct about everything she had told us. Last, he explained that my doctors were rushing the process by urging the feeding tube right away. He said, "They are not the ones who have to live with themselves if something goes wrong on the operating table."

The surgeon sent us home with the same message that the anesthesiologist had given us, to strongly reconsider the feeding tube surgery. My dad and I spent the entire ride home trying to make sense of the entire situation. I probably would have lost my mind had it not been for the McDonald's Sweet Tea I drank to soothe my nerves.

After that day at the hospital, my doctors and the surgical staff got into an email battle with both sides trying to convince each other that they were right. There was supposed to be a telephone conference in August to decide what to do, but that never happened because of a scheduling problem with all of the doctors. The doctor that had originally told me I needed a feeding tube has since retired, and made no attempt to resolve the situation or even contact us before she left. In fact, we didn't hear from any of those doctors for over a year.

I met with a new pulmonologist in Delaware the following summer. He was a really chill and understanding dude, but I had lost six pounds since my last checkup, bringing my weight to a whopping forty-six pounds, and he and I both knew a feeding tube was really my only option at this point. A few days later he wrote me a very convincing email explaining that he firmly believed, based on my life history and uncommonly high lung-function test scores, that I would have no problem coming off the breathing tube. He also reassured me that my doctors and surgeon were all on the same page this time, and I slowly accepted that a feeding tube was going to be a part of my future. I convinced myself that I would get through the surgery just fine.

The surgery was scheduled for the fall. At the pre-op meeting, the same surgeon from the previous summer made another complicating discovery. He realized how severe my leg contractures were. When I lie on my back, my legs are stuck in a "sitting" position. How he didn't notice this very obvious trait of mine last year is beyond me. Anyway, he was intensely troubled by this realization, because he explained, this made doing the surgery the way they had planned next to impossible. My legs would literally be in the way of the instruments that were vital to completing the surgery safely.

So there I was, lying on the examination table in my boxers, being poked and prodded by my surgeon and a female nurse who was obviously just there to try to get my number, chuckling out loud at how ridiculous my life is. How was this situation not funny? After all the mental gymnastics I'd done to psych myself up for the feeding tube surgery once again, and now I was being told there was another reason not to get it. Fucking fantastic.

My surgeon left the room and came back with some of his other surgeon friends. They all basically agreed that this new discovery made the surgery much more complicated. Then I had an idea, why not just use a nasal feeding tube? Some of the surgeons laughed when I tossed out the idea.

"You would have to keep it in your nose all the time, Shane," someone said.

"Why couldn't I just take it out every morning and put it in every night?" I asked.

The answer was basically because that has never been done before. Inserting a nasal feeding tube is very uncomfortable, surely I wouldn't want to do that. It suddenly seemed like the most obvious and perfect solution. I could deal with discomfort. I convinced them to let me at least try, arguing that I would most likely bite the dust if we didn't find a solution soon. They were hesitant, but made arrangements for me to be admitted to the hospital for a week-long crash course in nasal feeding tube insertion.

When I arrived at the hospital, I had to sign myself in, since it was the first time I was being admitted as an adult. The check-in lady informed me of my rights and told me I could discharge myself at any time. I turned my chair on and said, "All right, well I've had enough. I'm going to head out." She laughed in that "I-don't-know-if-this-kid-is-joking-or-mentally-disabled" kind of way.

The check-in lady walked my dad and me up to my room, which to my extreme pleasure did not have anyone else in the other bed. I had a pretty big room all to myself.

Within the first two hours of being in the room, I was interviewed by a nurse, a nurse-helper, a respiratory therapist, a pulmonologist, a student pulmonologist, a lead doctor-type dude, and a lead doctor-type dude's helper. They all asked me the same exact questions. Here is how most of the interviews went:

Doctor: So, Shane, tell me why you're here today. (I don't know why they all asked this, as if they didn't know.)

Me: I suck at gaining weight and the surgery to do the feeding tube is too dangerous right now, so I'm here to get set up with a nasal feeding tube, blah, blah, blah.

Doctor: Okay. Cool. So can you describe to me what you eat in a normal day, so we can get a sense of how many calories you normally take in?

Me: No. That question is too vague. Next question. (Not my real answer.)

Doctor: So I hear you have a Bi-PAP machine, but you're having some difficulties with it?

Me: Not difficulties, I just don't use it. (My real answer.)

Doctor: Okay, well we can work on that while you're here. Do you have an oxygen machine at home?

Me: Yup. Don't use it, though.

Doctor: How about your nebulizer?

Me: Only when I'm sick.

Doctor: Do you wear an oxygen monitor when you sleep?

Me: Have one. Don't use it.

Whenever new doctors ran me through this type of interview, they must have wondered if my parents neglected me, because I literally didn't use any of the normal medical devices that most other kids with SMA use, but the truth was I didn't need those devices and I was choosing not to use them. Maybe I partially just didn't want to accept that I needed them.

The lead doctor explained to me that they were going to take some blood to test my electrolytes and assess my overall level of nutrition, that way they could decide just how careful they needed to be when starting the overnight feedings.

Unfortunately, all of my veins are complete assholes, so it took the nurse a few stabs in both of my hands before she found a vein that yielded any blood. After that, I had a few hours to chill and eat dinner before they came back to put the feeding tube in for the first time. That night I had meat loaf and mashed potatoes that tasted like construction paper dipped in water.

Later, the main nurse came in and said she was going to put the feeding tube in. I don't know why, but I was kind of excited to get it over with. In my head, sliding the feeding tube down my nose into my stomach would be kind of uncomfortable, but nothing that I couldn't deal with. Wrong!

The nurse lubed up the end of the tube and stuck it in my right nostril, slowly working it to the back of my nose, and still I thought, "piece of cake!"

"Now," she said, "I have to get it past your airway so I need you to start swallowing and keep swallowing until I get it all the way in okay?" My expectations for how difficult it would be to overcome my gag reflex and swallow the tube were extremely flawed. On the first attempt, instead of sliding down my throat, the tube slipped into the back of my mouth, snaking out toward my lips. I choked. The nurse quickly pulled the tube all the way out. By this time I was sobbing, and it was completely involuntarily! I wasn't upset at all, more pissed than anything. Stick a piece of string into your nose right now and try to swallow it and you will understand why my eyes were watering so uncontrollably.

We failed in the same manner on the next three tries. Tube went in, eyes got real wide, demonic gagging noises, expression of panic, tube came out. After the fourth try I had to stop and collect myself for a few minutes. You know the feeling you get right before you throw up, where the world stops and you think, "SHIT, THIS IS IT"? I had that feeling times a hundred, but I was determined not to throw up. I blew the lube out of my nose into a tissue. My mom wiped my eyes, which were on fire at this point, and I mentally prepared myself to try again.

Finally, after two more failed attempts, I swallowed that son of a bitch into my stomach. But the fun was far from over. I also wildly underestimated how irritating the tube would be once it was in. It felt like there was a tiny animal clawing the walls of my throat every time I swallowed, talked, or moved. Great!

A tiny voice in the back of my head kept saying, "You're going to have to do this every fucking night from now on." I reasoned with myself that the first time was the worst and pretty soon I wouldn't feel the tube at all. I turned out to be right. Each night in the hospital became a little easier than the last. I started getting good at having the tube put in without gagging, and before I knew it I was home and back to my normal life, with the tiny difference of stopping to put the feeding tube in around 10 p.m. every night. This tube still scratches the back of my throat, but I've grown accustomed to the feeling. If I don't focus on it, the feeling disappears and I can sleep comfortably. However, I still choose to take the weekends off to give my nostrils and throat a break. No Feeding Tube Fridays have become a mini-holiday in my mind.

chapter 33

the amazing shannon o'connor

The feeding tube represents a long period of negativity and uncertainty in my life. I was scared and alone and quite fed up with the changes I had to make to continue to thrive. Shortly after becoming accustomed to the feeding tube, in the summer after my junior year, I met a girl who changed my life more than any one person ever has.

Upon writing this chapter in August 2013, we are dating. She is the girl I plan to marry.

But, Shane, how can you make such a grandiose claim in such a timeless place as a book? You're going to feel pretty stupid looking back on this if you don't end up marrying her.

Good point. I have no clue what's going to happen. For all I know, she could turn out to be a spy for the Russian government, who is almost certainly trying to shut down my blog and destroy any happiness I've created in the world. I could try heroin next week and slip into a vortex of devastating addiction, turning into a heartless monster that she could never learn to love. My lungs could give up and I could die in my sleep tomorrow or five or fifty years from now. She could get hit by a train.

Our futures are largely unpredictable.

All I know for sure is that if life goes the way I *want* it to, Shannon O'Connor from sunny Port Saint Lucie, Florida, will be the girl I spend the rest of my life with. It excites me to share that with the world in such a permanent way.

Our story is rather unusual, as most of mine are, and filled with millions of details that I could never begin to relate in a single book. This is my poor attempt to summarize our time together.

That is my "happiest boy on earth" face. Shannon and me being cute like always.

It started with a post on my blog in May 2012. My non-profit was looking for new volunteers. We had this crazy idea to make a mini-documentary about my life and how LAMN got started. For some terrible reason, we decided to crowd-source ideas for that documentary through the followers on my blog. In hindsight, it was probably the best worst idea I've ever had. Asking people from around the country who had little to no idea about who I was as a person to essentially storyboard a video about my life basically failed. (The final product was not a failure, though! Don't get ahead of me.) But I never would have met Shannon if it weren't for putting up a post asking for creative volunteers.

Her application stood out from the dozens of other "OMG YOU'RE MY HERO PLEASE LET ME WORK WITH YOU! <3" emails that I received. She wrote with refreshing honesty about the fact that her mom had passed away a few years prior due to an extensive battle with cancer. Witnessing her mom's long-term illness and eventual passing, she explained, taught her to appreciate every moment of being alive. She wanted to help share that message with the rest of the world.

This girl gets it.

As I read more, I was astonished when Shannon explained that she had graduated high school at the age of fifteen and was a freshman at Indian River State College by sixteen. Included in her application were several references and examples of work that she compiled from various internships she had balanced while attending school and helping to take care of her mom.

The profile picture associated with her email address further captivated me. She had a gentle smile, with bright eyes that radiated curiosity and wonder. Her lightly tanned, freckle-covered beach body grabbed hold of my mind and hasn't let go to this day. She was gorgeous.

This is not a fairy tale. There was no life-altering change inside of me while reading her application letter. I didn't rip my clothes off, climb a mountain, and announce to the heavens that I had found the girl of my dreams. Not that I even could if I felt so inclined.

My reaction was much more practical. This girl, who had a ton of creative experience in print and digital media, would obviously be a great asset to our video production team. I replied to her and a few other well-qualified candidates, congratulating them and initiating plans to begin working together. But later that night, I found myself rereading Shannon's email.

Fast-forward a few weeks. We were laughing. It was 8 a.m., and Shannon and I were already an hour into our first Skype of the day. Both of us looked like we desperately needed sleep, with baggy eyes and—for me at least—unshowered, crazy hair. We laughed quietly on either end of North America, careful to not wake anyone up in our respective houses, but giggled ourselves breathless nonetheless. I discovered soon after beginning to work with her that her sense of humor was flawless. We were always laughing. In this particular moment the laughter came from some of the more problematic ideas our creative team had generated. Someone suggested we do a remake of *The Lion King*, and Shannon was having trouble staying in her chair as she imagined me dressed up like a baby lion and lifted above someone's head, similar to the movie's opening scene.

It became apparent that Shannon was taking her volunteer position very seriously. I had expected to hold a brief Skype meeting with our creative team to introduce the project before sending them off to brainstorm on their own. I figured they'd submit their ideas via email and that would be the extent of our interaction. The process went as I imagined for all of our volunteers, except for Shannon, who was going to be more involved whether I wanted her to be or not. She gave me no option but to ask her for continued assistance throughout the rest of video production.

Shannon was having a rough time with a relationship that summer, explaining to me that over the previous few weeks, her boyfriend started to become a different person, one that was more interested in getting high than being in a committed relationship. I listened and did my best to let her know that I was there if she needed me, albeit a thousand miles away. At night, Skyping became less about work and more about getting to know each other. One day her boyfriend stopped replying to her texts and told her it was over four days before she was supposed to go on vacation to visit him.

On Skype that night, she hid her face and openly cried in front of me for the first time. It was devastating. I assured her there were better guys out there. As much as it pained me to see her so upset, it felt good to know that she was comfortable enough to share an intimate moment of her life with me. I desperately wanted to be next to her so she had someone to lean on. In that moment, I realized that I considered her my best friend.

We Skyped for hours on end that summer. My friends questioned why I had suddenly become a recluse. In years prior, my summers were spent lounging by the pool, going out with friends, and being outside as much as possible. I still did that stuff, but now my days were centered around Skyping with Shannon as much as possible. We worked on the video constantly. We texted incessantly. Along the way, I asked her to serve a larger role than the other volunteers who had helped with the video. When we weren't working, we told each other stories from childhood, made fun of people, discussed our lives and the future, and made each other laugh. Sometimes we ended up just sitting in silence on Skype together, an activity that never felt awkward to either of us.

Shannon suggested we reach out to local production studios for help with filming and editing the documentary. After many disheartening "Sorry, we are just too busy for a pro bono project at this time," responses, a company named FireRock Productions said they would love to get involved. A few meetings were held and filming was scheduled for late July. The night before filming, Shannon and I were on Skype discussing the shoot. One of the shots we were supposed to film the next day involved a slow-motion paint fight. Out of nothing but laziness and wanting to take the easy way out, I scrapped the idea without telling her. The shot required a bunch of supplies, and I didn't think the effort was worth the reward.

Shannon couldn't attend filming, since she lived in Florida, but she was involved in every last detail until the cameras were rolling. On Skype that night before filming, it came out that I wasn't planning to film the paint scene. She lost it. I was unprepared, and it suddenly felt like I had been thrown in a cage with a grizzly bear. In an argument that I feared would end with her never speaking to me again, she questioned my integrity, my character, and whether or not I had what it took to devote myself to LAMN wholeheartedly. I wanted to counter her stabbing questions with smart remarks and witty responses, but nothing came to me. She zeroed in on one of my biggest flaws with a level of perception that amazed me. By the end of our fight, I knew I needed to improve my dedication to the company. Shannon has never allowed me to accept complacency in any aspect of my life. She inspires and drives me to continually improve myself to be the best human being I can be.

We filmed the paint scene, and it was fucking awesome.

A few weeks later, I found myself crying uncontrollably in

Given the opportunity to take his shirt off, Andrew will always accept.

front of Shannon over Skype. I don't often cry, especially in front of other people, but that changed as well when Shannon came into my life. It was one of those rare moments when everything awful about my disease caught up to me all at once. I had woken up in the middle of the night, fairly certain that my body had just stopped breathing in my sleep. My lungs were obviously getting worse, which forced me to think about the fact that I am always getting worse and that it's never going to stop. Slowly but surely, I will lose all physical ability. Now my lungs were starting to fail, and I was afraid to go to sleep out of fear that I wouldn't wake up the next day.

I explained all of this to her through cloudy eyes and choked-back sobs.

"You're going to have good days and bad days," she reminded me, "and it's okay to be afraid." It was nice to hear that, and she was right.

The difference between Shannon and the rest of the world when talking about the issue of my disease, is that she doesn't make me feel like I need to change the subject as fast as possible for the sake of her own comfort. She is perfectly at home discussing my fears about death and the future.

We said good night, and I went to bed feeling considerably better than I did before.

A few nights later I told her I loved her, following with an addendum that I wasn't professing my romantic love to her (as much as I wanted to), but that I considered her one of my best friends, and should something bad happen to me, I needed her to know that I loved her in a best friend sort of way. I adopted a routine of texting her good night and I love you before bed every night. She began saying it back and everything seemed perfect. The first time I said it to her on Skype, the intensity of her blush-filled smile embarrassed her so much that she quickly said good night and hung up. I think we both began to sense deeper feelings that night.

On the morning of Friday, December 21, 2012—the day the world didn't end as some were predicting it might—my friend Pat came over in the morning to hang at my house for the day. His sister Erinn was getting married that night, so we figured we had at least five solid hours to play FIFA before he and my family had to get ready for the 7:30 p.m. service.

When Pat arrived, I was Skyping with Shannon, so he sat next to me and joined our conversation. Shannon and Pat were well acquainted by now. I had been talking to Shannon pretty much nonstop since I'd first met her back in May. Although we still hadn't met in person, she knew my friends and I knew her friends. After discussing the overwhelmingly disappointing Mayan apocalypse, we shared our plans for Christmas, as we were all very excited about the approaching holiday.

Pat and I would be partaking in our normal family traditions: visiting family, eating too much food, exchanging gifts, all the things that make Christmas such a beautiful time of year. Shannon, as she had been telling me for a few weeks, was flying by herself later that day to spend Christmas with family in Nevada. She was not looking forward to it, mostly because of her severe fear of flying, which is putting it lightly.

While we were Skyping, Shannon held her phone up to show me a funny picture. As she did this, I saw a notification flash on the top of her screen: "Text Message: Pat Hess." Oh cool, they were texting behind my back. I didn't care much; Pat had a girlfriend, and it was pretty well established that Shannon and I liked each other, but since I caught them in such a peculiar way, I pretended to get really mad and grilled Pat about what they were talking about. He awkwardly danced around my questions until I was sure they were talking about me, but he repeatedly assured me it was nothing, so I let it go. After a while, Shannon had to leave for the airport so we said goodbye and wished her good luck.

Pat and I played FIFA all day. Erinn's wedding was beautiful. When we came out of the church after the service, the night sky glittered with heavy snowflakes, which is about as romantic as you can get for a post-wedding scene. Life was pretty great, but I couldn't help but feel like I was missing something. Not having Shannon around to spend the holidays with just felt wrong. Although we lived so far apart, I considered her one of the most important parts of my life.

Later that night after the reception, Andrew and I were hanging in my room, planning on watching Netflix all night. Around 11:30 p.m. Andrew paused the movie and sheepishly said, "Hey, I think my friend Ryan is gonna come sleep over tonight, so I'm gonna have to go out and meet him cause he's never been here before."

I groaned, not really in the mood for his friend to intrude on movie night (mostly because I'd have to put pants on), and asked, "Ryan Patton? He's been here many times." Ryan was Andrew's best friend.

"No. Ryan Troxell. He's a new friend," he said. Then he stood up and left the room. While I waited, I checked my phone to see if Shannon had landed in Nevada yet, but she still hadn't responded to my text that I'd sent earlier that day. Bummer.

I sat in my room and ate leftover ravioli while impatiently waiting for Andrew and his new friend to come back. A few minutes later Andrew opened my door, came into my room, and said, "Hey, Shane, there's someone here that wants to see you."

Before I could even express confusion, Shannon walked into my bedroom.

No fucking way. No fucking way. No fucking way. My brain stopped working. I dropped my fork and stared at her in disbelief. She . . . Nevada . . . . flight . . . Bethlehem . . . she was standing in front of me . . . smiling . . . she came to Bethlehem! Thousands of thoughts and emotions flooded my mind, but all that came out was, "HOLY SHIT!"

Once we both got past the initial excitement of the fact that she was standing in my bedroom, she started explaining. She had been planning this trip for about a month. My parents, Andrew, Sarah, and my grandparents were all in on it. She came up with her stepdad, and they were staying until Christmas Day. I was in shock for at least the first two days.

Those four days with Shannon were some of the greatest days in my entire life. We hung out all day every day, and it felt like we'd been doing so our entire lives. She learned how to help me do many of the things I need help with (such as lifting me up, inserting the feeding tube, etc.) and met most of my family. We went sightseeing, made gingerbread houses, had a snowball fight, watched movies, played games, laughed, laughed, laughed, went ice skating, had Christmas dinner at my Nana's house, and made lots of fun of each other. It was perfect.

Shannon went back to Florida. About a month later on a

My job was to eat icing while watching Shannon build our gingerbread house.

terrifyingly cold night in January, we were on Skype, and this time both of us were crying. I fucked up big time.

For months I had been head over heels in love with Shannon. Nobody had ever made me as happy as she did and her Christmas surprise just made my desires for her a thousand times stronger. It was as if flying to Bethlehem made the possibility of us being together an actual reality.

She admitted to having very strong feelings for me on several occasions, but always added that she still wasn't ready to be with me. I told her I would wait because she was worth it to me. Shortly after she was back in Florida, we had the conversation again. She still felt the same way. I became discouraged. I knew she had many fears and hesitations about being in a relationship with me. They were justified and real and I understood them. But in my immature desire to have what I want when I wanted it, I began to lose sight of how much we loved each other. In essence, we were already dating without calling it that. Unfortunately, I couldn't handle being told once again that she wanted to be together but just wasn't ready yet, so I started talking to another girl. Perhaps it's fair to say that I began to doubt Shannon's feelings toward me and felt I needed to move on.

Back to us crying on Skype. Earlier that day, Shannon had asked me to Skype, as we usually did, but I told her I couldn't because I was talking with the new girl, and that things were going very well between us. Something let loose inside of her.

Reduced to tears in the library of her school, she asked with incredulousness if I really didn't believe she wanted to be with me. Had I forgotten everything we had been through? Was I ignoring everything we'd said to each other over the past year? Did I think her trip to Pennsylvania was something she'd have done for just anyone? Was I really going to throw away the profound love we shared for some immediate gratification?

I felt like the most horrible human to ever not walk the earth. Here I was, doubting her love, and when I tried to move on, I finally realized how serious she was about wanting to be together all along. Society tells me that I shouldn't admit to moments like this, but we sat on Skype together and bawled our eyes out. Sometimes she yelled and other times she could barely look at me she was crying so hard. I'm not sure which was worse. I was completely resigned. No apology could fix what I had done, but I apologized profusely anyway. In that moment, I realized I wanted to spend the rest of my life with Shannon, and that I would give anything to be together and make her happy. I will always regret upsetting her so deeply on that day.

It is summer, and Shannon and I are lying together watching a movie. Her head rests gently on my shoulder and I feel her steady breathing against my neck. I can't hide the perpetual smile whenever we are together. We are dating now and making regular trips to see each other. Shannon serves as the creative director for my nonprofit. We whisper in the darkness about what we are going to do as my condition worsens down the road. We are planning out our future together. I should be terrified. My future is a very scary idea, but all I feel is confidence. Her hand tucks perfectly into mine and we lie quietly for a while, just holding hands.

"We will figure it out—together," she says, "No matter what happens we are going to get through it together."

I believe her.

For most of my life, as I mentioned, I have not been in a wheelchair in my dreams. In them I run and jump and play sports, and when I wake up, I wish I could fall back asleep and return to that perfect world without my chair. A few months after meeting Shannon, those dreams stopped, and now I'm in a wheelchair in all of my dreams. I'm no expert, but I believe that at a subconscious level, my body no longer desires the escape of being able to walk.

There's no better way for me to capture our relationship in writing. Shannon O'Connor makes me excited about our long-term future and gives me incredible comfort in dealing with my disease and everything it brings.

This was taken seconds after Shannon farted.

chapter 34

the end (the beginning)

The floor of the living room in our house is strewn with cardboard boxes overflowing with Laughing at My Nightmare merchandise, suitcases, camera bags, lighting equipment, coolers, and about a thousand other things. Mom sits on the couch, glancing anxiously back and forth between a list in her hands and the mounds of crap on the floor.

"You are absolutely positive you have everything?" she asks me for the seventh time.

"One hundred percent," I say, staring out the front window at the white rented minibus that's being loaded from the rear. The first annual Laughing at My Nightmare LaughTour begins tomorrow.

We wake up with the sun on May 24, 2013. Andrew comes into my room to get me dressed and seems more excited than I do, but to be fair, I still haven't had my coffee, and yesterday was his last day of high school. That's really where this whole crazy idea came from. Andrew and I decided we wanted to do something epic to celebrate our last summer together before he went off to college. A road trip to visit Shannon in Florida seemed like the perfect adventure. Mom wasn't so hot on the idea of Andrew keeping me alive on the road, and requested we bring a third person along. I invited my friend Mark Male, who was serving as the Operations Director for my nonprofit at the time. We were originally connected through a mutual friend just a few months before, but had become great friends in that brief amount of time. He agreed, and Mom gave us the go-ahead. Mark, Andrew, Shannon, and I began to scheme. What if, instead of just driving to Florida to visit Shannon for a few days, we picked her up and did a Laughing at My Nightmare speaking tour on the way back to Pennsylvania? We took hold of this idea and ran with it.

The details started to fall together as if by magic. Putting a post on my blog was enough to get us speaking engagements at three venues, including one speech to the employees of Disney World. We arranged and began to promote four additional Meet-Ups (where supporters could come hang with us for a few hours) at Panera Bread locations in four states along the way. Earlier in the year, Rainn Wilson's company, Soulpancake had done a documentary about my life and the blog, so I reached out to their film crew to see what they thought about doing a full-length documentary on the trip. They loved the idea, and we began to crowdsource funding to make it possible for them to come.

"The film crew is already here," says Andrew, rolling me out of bed. Justin, the director, sneaks into my room followed by two cameramen and a sound technician. They capture Andrew putting shorts and a T-shirt on me as we prepare for our first road trip without our parents.

"I'm not doing this again until we get home, so I hope you like these clothes," Andrew says to me. Justin stifles a laugh, but not very well.

I look directly into the camera Justin is holding and say, "You're gonna have to get better at controlling your laughter or you're going to ruin the whole documentary, asshole."

"You're gonna have to not look at the camera or talk to me while we're filming, stupid" he says.

"You can suck a dick and not come with us," I say. Now the whole crew is laughing and the rest of the shot is mostly ruined. This becomes a theme during the trip, trying to make the film crew laugh to mess up their shots.

I say goodbye to my parents in the gentle rain of the early summer morning. Mom is nervous, still making sure we have everything. Dad is cautiously excited. Two vans depart from our cul-de-sac, one driven by Mark, with Andrew, me, and two cameramen inside, and another with the rest of the crew. Next stop: Daytona Beach, Florida.

We all underestimate how boring the first leg of the drive is going to be. The interviews start as soon as we're on the highway. Justin questions all of us about everything from our sexual fantasies to our expectations for the trip as we cruise down I-95. When filming a documentary in a car, you can't have the windows open or the radio on, or the noise ruins the shots. This becomes highly annoying around hour five or six. Andrew gets bored and starts farting to entertain himself as we gag in the windless van. Despite the small annoyances, this is by far the most fun I've ever had.

We get to our hotel room in Daytona Beach around 3:30 a.m. Andrew is driving when we arrive, but the only reason we've made it in one piece is because I've been screaming at him to stay awake for the past two hours. The motel room has to be the most disgusting things I've ever seen. It's still ninety-eight degrees and 100 percent humidity in Florida at 3:30 a.m., and the hotel room feels like the inside of an old man's crotch. And it's full of bugs. We are so tired we hardly even care. The schedule Mark and I created for the trip says we need to be back on the road by 6 a.m., so Andrew tosses me into bed and we crash for a few precious hours. (Thank God I decided to opt out of using the feeding tube on this trip, so we could avoid that whole procedure and go right to sleep.)

We arrive at Shannon's house midmorning the next day. I can't get over how oppressively hot it is outside. I love it. Everyone else complains incessantly about the sweat gathering in their underwear. I ignore the sweat and drink up the beautiful sun. Shannon practically cartwheels out to meet us, hugging everyone, including the film crew who she has met only on Skype to this point. We are a great big family already. After a quick but gracious breakfast with her family, we are back on the road. Shannon's ridiculous amount of clothing barely fits in the van. We almost have to leave her behind.

At our first Meet-Up in Orlando, we realize we should have made more concrete plans with the staff at Panera. About fifteen people show up to meet us, and the restaurant is so busy that we have tremendous trouble finding a place for everyone to sit. Lack of room doesn't dampen anyone's enthusiasm, though. A man in his late twenties, covered in tattoos, with a backward cap, begins to cry as he thanks me for writing my blog and starting the nonprofit to continue sharing the message of humor. "You helped me get through some tough shit, man," he says to me. I'm overwhelmed. This is suddenly so real. The implication of the work Shannon and Mark and I have been doing finally hits me. I sound like a babbling idiot as I try to thank him in return, knowing I can never show him how happy he has made me.

On the way to Disney, Shannon surprises me once again. She has reserved us a room at a fancy resort in Disney for the two nights we are staying there. "Happy Birthday!" she says. I have almost forgotten that I turn twenty-one in just three days. The room is amazing, but not quite as amazing as the lake, the pool, the bonfires, the scenery, the candy, and all the food I can imagine that comes with staying at this resort. Shannon loves Disney either equally or more than she loves me, and she isn't settled in the room for two minutes before she asks when we are going to Magic Kingdom.

Our speech to the Disney employees is the next day, and

when we arrive they tell us no professional film crews are permitted inside the park. Personal cameras are fine. Easy enough, we strap a Canon 5D Mark 3 to the headrest of my wheelchair, and my "personal camera" records every minute of our day. There aren't many amusement park rides I can go on without snapping in half, so we take our time exploring the park. Mark and Shannon and some of the film crew ride a few roller coasters, but most of the time we stick together.

The speech goes better than we expect it to go, since it is our first. The cast members surprise us, and we get to speak to a group of about fifty employees inside Cinderella's castle. After that, they announce that the four of us have been chosen to lead the big parade through Magic Kingdom that afternoon. Thousands of people line the streets of Disney as we ride in the Grand Marshal's car through the park. Justin sprints through the crowd trying to capture it on his "personal camera." By the time we get back to the hotel late that night, everyone is too dead to do anything but relax by the pool. I am in paradise.

We stop for another Meet-Up in the stunningly beautiful city of Savannah, Georgia, before moving on to Charlotte, where we stay at Mark's house for a quick night. I turn twenty-one at midnight, and Mark's roommate bakes a cake. I take my first legal shot of Jack Daniels. The film crew captures me pooping and also films the clean up process that night. Normally, this would have been the most awkward moment of my life, but I'm so tired I don't even care. That night I fall asleep harder than I ever have before. As much

The Laughing at My Nightmare crew and part of the documentary team.

fun as we are having, this is by far the most exhausting experience of my life.

In the morning we depart at the crack of dawn for a morning Meet-Up in downtown Charlotte. We are half an hour late, but when we enter, a teenage girl and her mom leap from their table to greet us. They tell us they have FLOWN FROM ALABAMA TO ATTEND THIS MEET-UP! The girl, Lillie-Ben, says she found my blog while going through a tough time, and that my story helped her get through her adversity. She has a necklace for me, that is meant to be passed on to someone who impacts you deeply. I am honored. I ask them probably ten times if they seriously got on a plane just to see me. We hang with them and the many other awesome people who are there for as long as we can, but soon must pile back in the van to travel to our next speech in Winston-Salem, North Carolina.

I fall asleep in the van facedown into a pillow that I situate in front of me in my wheelchair. When I wake up, I'm covered in gooey drool. Shannon cleans me up and teases me relentlessly before we head into the high school that we're speaking at.

We are an hour early. The stage at the front of the empty auditorium has five massive steps keeping me from getting where I need to be. We forgot my portable ramps at home, the only item to escape Mom's anal list checking. After greeting us, the principal of the Kingswood school departs from the auditorium to round up a group of hulking men. Together they lift my wheelchair onto the stage while I lie on my back across three auditorium seats. Andrew carries me up the steps and puts me back in my wheelchair, helping to hide my wireless mic discreetly behind shoulder straps. I'm getting nervous as we make last-minute preparations backstage. Our speech, which Mark, Shannon, and I have been writing and rehearsing for the past month, seems like a foreign language, I can't remember any of it. Between a gap in the curtain I see the auditorium filling up with hundreds of students. My heart is racing, and the muscles in my jaw start to constrict. I fear I won't be able to speak for very long before I'm reduced to an indecipherable mess. The three of us share a collective moment of panic as we realize we don't know the speech well enough to give it without the use of notes. We decide to have the speech open on a laptop, in case we forget our place.

The crowd erupts as we are presented and come into the spotlight. Holy shit, why? They are treating us like superstars. Surely we won't live up to their expectations. Deep breaths, I tell myself. Don't focus on your tightening jaw. Just talk. We begin, and our opening lines illicit genuine laughter. I expect a school full of troubled youth couldn't care less about what we have to say, but they are focused intently on us, so much that it's almost creepy. Much of the rest of the speech is a blur. My jaw starts to act up, and I work through it. Shannon forgets a line, and the audience doesn't even notice. Mark, who had the least amount memorized, barely needs to use his notes. At the end, the audience erupts again. The students start a standing ovation and Shannon cries. I tear up as well, but I'm a tough macho man so I hide it as best I can.

During the Q&A that immediately follows the speech, near the end, one of the younger students from the middle school stands to ask a question. He is maybe thirteen, with shaggy clothes and a rough look that tells me he hasn't had an easy life. His friends look at him in awe, as if this is completely unlike him.

Proudly and confidently he looks up to us and says, "I just want to thank you guys for coming to our school and sharing your story. I have a lot of problems myself, and hearing your story and the way you handle your problems makes me want to write my story down to share with people and to look at life more positively like you guys do."

His words hit me like train. My entire life I have been striving to convince the world that I am normal, that my disease doesn't define me. Now, here stands a little kid who is thanking me for just being me and sharing my story with him. I could've gotten on that stage and spouted an hour of "People in Wheelchairs Are Normal!" and it probably wouldn't have affected a single person in that auditorium. Instead, the three of us spoke honestly about our lives. None of us are normal. I have a disease that's causing my muscles to waste away. I don't know if I'll be alive in ten years. I'm afraid to die. There are tons of annoying, aggravating, obnoxious, and difficult things about living with SMA. But you know what? Life is still fucking awesome. Every single one of us has problems. That's part of being alive. The beauty begins when you connect with other people and realize that we're all in the same boat. Once we accept that life is inherently difficult, we can move on and focus on having a good time despite the tough stuff.

Until now I believed my blog and the nonprofit were just ways to make people laugh, a form of entertainment. I received countless emails telling me how much I was helping people, and I became numb to it! There's no way a story about spilling urine on myself is actually going to change anyone's life. But the genuine gratitude in this kid's voice has slapped me across the face and opened my eyes. I thank him, but my words don't come close to expressing how profoundly he has impacted me. The curtain closes behind us as we head backstage to pack up for the drive to the next stop.

I've come a long way in my twenty-one years, but I'm nowhere close to slowing down. As I get older, my body will continue to get worse until I lose even the tiny bit of freedom that I have now, but you better believe that's not going to stop me.

I will throw everything I have into this life for as long as I can physically manage. Maybe it'll be a huge failure. If, at the end of it all, I can look back and know that I made some people laugh, it will have all been worth it.

Now, how to end this? Uhh . . . wanna know how I poop?

How I Poop:

Step 1: Dad lifts me from wheelchair to changing table he made for our bathroom. (It's really just a floor cabinet with a soft pad on top.)

Step 2: Dad pulls my shorts and boxers off.

Step 3: Dad lifts me from changing table to toilet and straps me into special backrest. Dad leaves bathroom.

Step 4: I poop by contracting the muscles in my rectum.

Step 5: I yell, "DONE!" when I'm done. Sometimes when I'm feeling fancy, I sing it.

Step 6: Dad lifts me back onto changing table. (Occasionally, there is what we call "a hanger," also commonly referred to as a "dingleberry." If a hanger is present, lifting must be executed with extreme caution.

Step 7: Dad wipes my ass with a baby wipe while I pretend to be macho.

Step 8: Dad redresses me and puts me back in my chair.

Step 9: I exit the bathroom and announce the size of my poop to all present family members and houseguests.

acknowledgments

Fear of accidently leaving someone out almost caused me not to write acknowledgments. This list is by no means exhaustive. There are an incredible number of people who have helped me along the way. I am forever grateful to each of you, whether I name you here or not.

First, I would like to thank my parents and brother for putting up with me through this writing experience. We all know that I sometimes got pretty moody after days of writing and editing. Your support and encouragement, toward my book and my life in general, mean the world to me, and I can never say thank you enough for being so amazing. Andrew, I'm still cooler than you. Thank you to my girlfriend, Shannon, for believing in me and daring me to step outside my comfort zone when I write. Thank you to my extended family for your genuine interest in all of my activities, from this book to the nonprofit. Thank you to my friends for not hating me too much when all I could think about was writing. A very special thank you goes to Joyce Hinnefeld, a professor of mine who became my mentor for this whole writing process. Your coaching and honest reviews of my drafts made this book about a million times better. Thank you to my friend Paul Acampora for introducing me to the amazing Tina Wexler at ICM, who became my agent. On that note, thank you Tina for not rejecting my initial query. It still blows my mind that you wanted to represent me. Your guidance has made this so much more enjoyable. Last but not least, thank you to my brilliant editor, Nancy Mercado, who challenged me and refused to let me put anything but my best into these pages.

When this book goes double platinum I'll buy you all a beer. Can books go platinum?